Time for Somerset

by

Diana Crighton

EXCURSION PUBLISHING

Other titles by Diana Crighton

- Visiting with Taste
- English Excursions, Home Counties and London
- English Excursions, Northern Journey

Cover painting by kind permission of Sue Onley
Illustrations and map Mark Smith
All photographs Diana Crighton
Design: Global Image - *mike.globalimage@btinternet.com*
Printed by J. H. Haynes & Company Ltd., Sparkford, Somerset
Published by Excursion Publishing, Somerset
www.timeforsomerset.co.uk

ISBN 0-9528334-2-5

Acknowledgements

There are many people who have helped me during the research for this book. I would like to thank the staff at the local Somerset libraries I use across the county; David Bromwich and colleagues at Somerset Studies, and the County Record Office, Taunton; also David Buri librarian at Glasgow School of Art; the Elgin Heritage Centre and museum; Charles Hind, Curator of Drawings RIBA and Dr William Whyte, St John's College, Oxford. I owe a debt to the honorary curators of Somerset's small museums, in particular: Dennis Corner, Ben Norman and John Nash; to John Bishton of Bruton Civic Society and the clerk of the Priddy parish council. The staff at the Porlock Information Centre have been tireless. I am also grateful to the offices of the Bath and West and Shepton Shows and the cheesemakers.

Many more have given their help and shared information: Rosemary Burnett; Richard Clark; Nick and Lynda Cotton; Jennifer Dagworthy; Sue Farrington; John and Mary Hecks; Angela Hesselgren; Keith and Pam Johnson; Gilly March; Tony and John Richards; Dr Eric Robinson; Jerry Sampson and Malcolm Scott. I feel privileged to have been welcomed into so many houses for research purposes and my dear friends will know how much I value their support.

For Alison

Contents

Page

Map of Somerset

Chapter 5

Chapter 6

Chapter 7

Chapter 8

Introduction

In this clock-watching, minute-minding society, making excuses for not seeing or experiencing the simple delights of life is too easy.

My delight is in the phenomena of the everyday; especially the sunsets over Glastonbury Tor or reflected in the medieval windows of the Chain Gate at Wells Cathedral; and then the fiery finish from the beach at West Quantoxhead, as it dips into the sea behind North Hill.

I am seduced by Somerset, its geology and weather, the mists rolling over the Mendip Hills and Exmoor. I am as engrossed in the passing of the seasons, the 'intimacies of winter' and the 'prosperities of summer', the first cut, the first house martins, as those who farm, create gardens and practice their crafts are inspired by a love of the land.

'Most men are so careful of time they dare not pause to enjoy idling, to taste to the full the pleasure of simple things.' Not so in the case of Walter Raymond, the Somerset folk collector and novelist of the 1920s who found pleasure in such delights, and won the above praise from Evelyn Clark.

Unearthing the unusual has always been my ploy. Somerset delivers. Somerset's traditions are alive — wassailing, harvest suppers, street fairs and hundreds of children enjoying country dancing on Wells' Cathedral Green.

I follow in the footsteps and make comparisons with earlier topographical writers who walked along turnpike roads; the eighteenth-century writers William Maton, Richard Warner and

William Gilpin. And, more romantically, the poet Samuel Taylor Coleridge and his friends William Wordsworth and William Hazlitt.

In this cause I dare readers to hop on the bus at Dunster and experience another Exmoor as the road twists and follows three rivers to Dulverton. Leave the car and take the train to Frome or to the county town of Taunton. Look at architecture and discover history, or in a more level mode, walk and meet the endless charm of Muchelney.

No passport needed! Just board the West Somerset Railway from Bishops Lydeard to see the Somerset coast at Minehead and beyond and the art and idiosyncrasies of Watchet. Surprisingly, bus and train journeys are liberating; in some cases it may take a little longer, but country conversation and new friendships with fellow passengers are not found in the car.

Dispense with any preconceived lists when you go shopping along lanes, past farm gates, to a clutch of Somerset village produce markets — Drayton, Barrington and Kingsbury Episcopi, or to the age-old weekly town markets. At agricultural shows you will come face to face with a healthy interest in growing, showing, craft, baking and beekeeping. Country arts are being revived.

Somerset remains a county of unexpected encounters: mine have ranged from meeting a solitary man milking his cows on the levels to the dedicated volunteers restoring the station at Williton on a winter's day. In this small world I meet wonderful characters and experience unending coincidences that make me feel part of this county.

My collection is rooted in the vernacular, in the food, (the best is usually served at farmhouses and at homely tables), and in the diverse architecture and extraordinary landscape that Somerset possesses.

I urge readers to come off the main roads and explore some of the many parish churches I happen upon. Collect the key for

Langport, look at the sculpture and stained glass at Mells and marvel at Dunkery Beacon from the south porch at Selworthy. Naturally, Wells the most beautiful cathedral in the country and the much visited ruins of Glastonbury Abbey, are in this selection.

But seekers of modern and twentieth-century architecture may also be reassured. I have found unrecorded examples and one true Somerset first. In 1947, the year after this country's first Arts Centre opened at Bridgwater, Somerset hosted the sixth annual C.I.A.M congress to which the gods of modernism came from all over the world. Here in the theatre, Le Corbusier, Walter Gropius, Alvaar Alto and their English counterparts, debated, among other papers, a policy of social housing for the town. Bridgwater might have acquired a modernist reputation. What a provoking thought!

My continuing search for the past — how it informs, influences and inspires the present, in art, architecture, farming and customs — has proven the pressing need to cherish; whether it is an old sign, a doorway, willow crops, artisan cheeses, or the dialect of our indigenous people. These are the constituents of Somerset's surprising identity, culture and independent nature. Get under the skin of this wonderful county and before long you will also find yourself in the slow, and inevitably more interesting, lane of life.

'Every detail of country life offers convincing proof of its skills to anyone who cares to look'. Go looking; visit the tourist information centres; collect all the timetables; take off, discover, and I hope you enjoy as much as I have!

Chapter 1

Frome: a town with charisma

*From Great Elm a river walk,
    Mells and a village garden*

Nunney: a village with a castle

Frome: a town with charisma

We start at Frome. I have a particular fondness for what was my first Somerset port of call on my way to work on a project in Wells. Here I saw the first signpost to Somerset's contemporary artists. Later I discovered some of Frome's extraordinary architectural heritage – a banquet one could never hope to do justice to. But there is more: over recent years a successful, and growing, arts festival whets the appetite for another course!

The buildings are fascinating evidence of the weaving industry in the 1690s, and the observations that Daniel Defoe made in 1726, with an astute businessman's eye, ring true. He wrote that if it continued to grow, it was likely to be the greatest and wealthiest inland town in England. His Froom or Frome Sellwood, with its new streets of houses built for the cloth makers, is, indeed, a rare example of this period in this country; in fact it is the only such industrial town in Somerset.

Defoe, being a nonconformist, naturally noted the 'numerous meeting houses' and churches. Some have been re-used and in one important case, the Rook Lane Chapel of 1707, creatively restored to provide an arts exhibition space, with an architect's practice on the first-floor gallery. Without doubt the architecture of these dissenting chapels has added a rich diversity to the Frome streetscape.

Frome's pre-medieval history begins with St Aldhelm's founding mission in 685, on which the parish church of St John, Norman with some earlier Celtic carvings, was later built; its important features are Victorian sculpture, a wrought-iron screen by Singers of Frome in 1863 and the tomb of Bishop Ken — the composer of many well-loved hymns, including 'Glory to Thee my God' — who, sadly, has an unremarkable grave.

Nearby there is Gentle Street (named after the family) and the beginning of a wonderful walk. It is the prelude to any number of climbs, cobbled and pedestrian streets, and secreted corners. Once, this was the main exit or arrival for the London coach. It would leave the Waggon and Horses, halfway up, among several fine houses, every Monday. Notably, Argyll House has a double dose of Venetian windows. But the street is Gentle in name only. It is cobbled with a very steep gradient and no longer takes coaches.

If you walk down Bath Street past Sir Jeffry Wyatville's screen in front of St John's, you can see the reasoning behind the street's original design. It was built by Thomas Bunn in 1810 with the intention of providing an elegant area for shopping whilst making the coach access easier than Gentle Street or Rook Lane. It was named after the landlord, Lord Bath, and has been called a brave piece of planning for a town of this size by Mark Girouard. At first-floor level, the windows and remaining shop signs give us an idea of the street's former style. One of the first shops was Butler and Langford — who added a small printing section to print their pharmacy labels — the forerunner of Butler and Tanner. In 1854 they advertised 'teas and coffee, for ready money', and a 'West of England sauce' — what was this, I wonder?

Now there is a choice: either a second climb like this one up Catherine Hill or continue through the Market Place and look at Cheap Street. The former was one of the principal shopping streets until comparatively recently, now it is the latter which has the bustle. At street level below the sixteenth-century merchants' houses, every trader keeps their own style. However entrepreneurs of all ages have seen the possibilities of opening a business on Catherine Hill, so that slowly but surely vitality is coming back. Cayfords, still called 'family butcher', is the only surviving butcher's shop, though once there were fourteen in this street. I half expected to see brown paper carrier bags hanging up on hooks, as they once did in every butcher's. They could not be more local, selling Somerset game, lamb and beef. A picture framer and a pint size deli are also restoring some life among the empty shops.

Cheap Street has a central conduit and below the merchants' houses there are wonderful bakers, clothes and jewellery, a greengrocer with a sophisticated array, a bookseller, gifts, splendid whole-foods and a speciality local food shop. At the junction of King Street and Church Street there is a fabric and textile shop where I have seen books of art history on the large counter. They have a beautiful collection, which includes materials from some of the last English silk mills. Frome also has its own family-run auction house called Dore and Rees just above in Vicarage Street — in business since 1868. I try to choose Wednesday for the weekly market when it coincides with the auctioneer's fortnightly sales of effects.

Window in
Christchurch Street

The seventeenth-century urban estate named 'the Trinity' puts the whole of the above in context. Fortunately much of this quarter was saved in 1976, following threatened demolition, by a strong public appeal and support in the year when architectural heritage was being blazoned. Frome now has around 350 listed buildings and it is worth taking the guided town walks with historian Bob Ladd to see these. Many have been recorded in detail: they are spacious, some are fifty feet wide, with carved shell cupboards or chimneypieces and decorative door furniture.

Descending narrow Whittox Lane from where Catherine Hill changes, there is another chapel and Melrose House, arguably the finest in the town. At some period the seventeenth-century side windows onto the lane were blocked, leaving the exterior stone mullions, whilst the best side has later Queen Anne windows with shutters and, above the windows, interior painted panels. Many of these houses have fine walled gardens and whole streets have been restored.

Out of the way
and out of the ordinary

Any of the roads leading from Christchurch Road West are worth taking to see more, and the whole restored Vallis Way; number five has an oval medallion stair window. And then there is Castle Street where an adjacent public house, no name, has original wooden window bars without glazing in an outbuilding. Frome is not all polished, with thankfully, a degree of what I call crumbliness being a constituent of its charisma. And it is worth exploring the Bartons or courts, which often lead to small hidden squares. These alleys are frequently named after landlords who took leases and built houses for their workers.

In Trinity Street, which has some examples of 1690s gable-end houses, the growing population warranted a new church, built in 1837, which squares off the street elegantly. This is not high Victorian, the west front built in the Commissioners' style. There are no aisles. It was designed by H.E. Goodrich, who had worked in the 1820s on Beckford's Tower in Bath and he followed this work with the Roman Catholic pro-cathedral church of the Holy Apostles in Clifton, Bristol. Later, in the 1880s, some of the stained glass in the north and south windows was designed by Edward Burne-Jones for Morris & Co.

Back at the market place one of the notable buildings, on the bridge, is The Blue House of 1720–8, which has a stunning façade — a rebuild of a medieval almshouse. From here a detour to Willow Vale provides a pastoral interlude, where one finds slender Queen Anne houses and beautiful porches by the water. Across at the corner of Bridge Street and North Parade, the Scientific and Literary Institute stands and has become the new location for the town museum that has a growing collection of diaries and industrial history. The Institute was also built through the vision of Thomas Bunn in 1869, in Ruskinian Gothic style.

Markets have always played an important part in Frome's commercial history and still do. Between 1500 and 1888 Somerset had more markets than any other west country county, for cloth, livestock and cheese. In addition to the famous one-day Cheese Show, now held outside the town, there are two public market days: one on Wednesday with fish, organic vegetables and flower stalls being set out in the Market Place; and there is a much larger range of goods, such as haberdashery, unavailable in shops today, local food, fish and cheese, in the Old Cattle Market, also here on Saturdays. There is the added bonus of a substantial country market held in the Cheese and Grain hall on Thursdays with all the usual baked and preserved country delights, whilst some of the best plants and garden flowers are laid out 'just so' on long bolts of hessian; their plants did me very well in my first Somerset garden. As if this were not enough to tickle the taste buds, Frome Farmers' Market has been increased to a twice-monthly outing. These successes must owe much to Frome being the largest town in the Mendip area and it being on a railway line to Bath.

In July, an arts festival floods the town's well- and less-well-known venues: performances take place in their two theatres, Community College and library. Poetry and folk music happen in out-of-the-way pubs — the Griffin in Milk Street still makes its own beer. However throughout the year there is a superabundance of art being created in and around Frome *sotto voce*. Frome is seething with makers and never fails to surprise me; its unexpectedness is an endearing quality.

Following the earlier success of cloth, Frome's craftsmen made stained glass and metalwork. The skill of J.W. Singer's workforce — one of Frome's most important nineteenth-century industries — was also in metalwork. Singers made candlesticks for Oxford Colleges; the camel for General Gordon's statue, (which required a whole new shed for the vast cast), and Boudicca, her horses and the figure of Justice, high above the law courts, all in London.

Firing at varying degrees of heat is the process of fixing another art form being practised in and around Frome. Many ceramists have trained at Frome College's well-attended course led by Russell Coates. And several of his former students now have their own studios further afield and all over the Mendips. One is Jane Evans who pots at Ditcheat — from her I bought a cool celadon pot. Coates's own work spreads internationally, but is probably not as well respected locally as it deserves to be. It has been exhibited throughout the country; he initiated the Potfest in Frome and earlier at Penrith, and recently designed and hand-painted restaurant tiles for the liner Aurora. He has also been commissioned by Spode, where he was artist in residence. Frome's contemporary ceramic history is rich: Hans Coper lived in Frome for thirteen years between 1967 until he died in 1981; his wife still lives in the town of Frome.

Finding Frome's art is an onionskin exercise — you have to be patient. Peel away slowly and all manner of talent is revealed. And so it was down-along-a-Barton where I met a maker who weaves willow and scavenged garden strands — maybe privet, blackberry or ivy — into her baskets, giving them a luminous texture; others, much softer, are in flax and dried phormium leaves. She also makes rag rugs, for which she needs, again, to scavenge for ends and scraps of material.

Black Swan Arts occupies one of the earliest eighteenth-century inns on Frome's north side. They have a large craft shop and gallery selling, and often showing, the work of local and regional artists. The range of outbuildings, that contain working studios, have been brought together and the whole site, including the Round Tower — a former cloth-drying mill — is used for exhibitions and the Tourist Information Centre. Panels of blue glass were commissioned from Anne Smythe for the entrance doors and a further etched window lets light into the inner dining room.

Part of the organisation's ongoing mission is to promote local makers whose own contemporary craft practice is rooted in the Somerset traditions of the past. Among these are the stone carver Kate Semple, a teacher at Shute Farm Studios at Downhead,who amalgamates stone, wood and glass, the building materials, we see every day; Rebecca Board, whose baskets demonstrate how willow and Somerset are inseparable; Ama Bolton's three-dimensional felt pieces and work by the potter Mark Melbourne.

Little did I know when I first visited Black Swan Arts, years ago, that this would lead to many exciting visits to artists in their studios, scattered across the hills and moors of Somerset, about whom I have written, and whose work I have been enticed to collect, in a very minor way.

From Great Elm a river walk, Mells and a village garden

Before the days of cars, the residents of Frome would walk across a field to Vallis Vale by the River Mells, a favourite destination and still an idyllic one. Nearby, over the last few years, the Jackdaw Music Education Trust has not only put on concerts and recitals, but also, through their workshops and camps, reached the wider community. Their programme gives children — some with disabilities, some who may never have even heard classical music before — the chance to sing Monteverdi in Latin, which was a great success, or to take part in a production of *The Magic Flute* in costume.

At the other end of the village, at Hapsford House, over some sixteen years a wildlife garden was made like no other. The owner has restored and developed the garden so that it became a rare example. A contemporary response to landscape gardening. Both the restoration and the new elements were made under the direction of Pam Lewis of Sticky Wicket and in close partnership with their own gardeners.

Vallis Vale, a dreamy destination by the River Mells

Over a handful of high-summer days visitors have been able to enjoy the trees that have been added to the monumental broad-leaf native species of oak, beech, ash, hornbeam, lime and willow. Like others, I drifted through the wildflower meadows have become rich habitats for a multitude of different species.

In this garden every felled trunk has been delightfully crafted into seating or gates and the bark used for mulch. Branches were used to support roses and wayward plants, and to protect young trees. With each successive visit I have seen how nature has been nurtured and coaxed with a gentle grasp.

However it is the island or aptly named *flowery mead* that is most magical, memorable and arresting; with wild hot pink campion, centaurea and geraniums all shimmering in their enclosure of river and woodland. One almost wonders if its brief *apogée* is a dream or reality. I felt that the curving paths, birdsong, poppies in every stage of bloom, foxgloves with romantic untrammelled roses are not so much designed to take all the attention, rather they were the supporting cast, contributing to the exceptional mood that Hapsford inspired.

On one visit, almost on cue as my daughter and I stood by the bridge and moored boat, a fly past of blue kingfishers skimmed the bank. In June, before the first cut, the wildflowers provide food for many butterflies — such as ringlet, speckle and silver-washed fritillaries — and elsewhere the stunning metallic blue damselflies and mayflies.

The success is Hapsford's planting contrasts: of shaded wood, sun-drenched meadows, the refreshing effect of wind-stirred leaves — all choreographed without artifice.

A walk along the river brings one to Mells, an historic village, once owned by the Benedictine monks of Glastonbury — an eastern outpost. John Horner was the bailiff just before the Reformation and the very rich plum of an estate — ostensibly giving rise to the nursery rhyme — was bought by Thomas Horner, whose descendants still own most of Mells.

The fascination of Mells is that it had all the makings of a 'praty townelet' — a small medieval town planned in 1470 by Abbot Selwood. His notion, to build four streets that would meet in the Roman cruciform fashion, could be described as early Renaissance. New Street, the northerly and only element actually built, leads from the main Selwood or High Street to the church but was not actually aligned with the porch or vestry. It is terraced on both sides with limestone roof-tiles, each house having a room either side of the front door, and a spiral staircase in a polygonal annexe at the rear. With windows of such diverse style and age — one now blocked has a carved trefoil arch — this façade is worthy of detailed sketching. One wonders if there was a shop among the houses. Thus the medieval core of Mells is like no other in Somerset, the nearest being the Vicars' Close in Wells, built for a different reason some years earlier.

A 15th Century window in Selwood Street

Six different roads lead to Mells, rife with river-walks, charming cottages, fine houses and memorials. And in March there is more to delight when every bank, border and bluff, planted with thousands of daffodils, are in flower and if the weather is kind they are in bloom for the Easter Monday Daffodil Festival.

From one of the banks opposite the Manor House, once perhaps Abbot Selwood's Grange, is a view to wonder at. Near the five Elizabethan-looking gable dormers of the Manor, the 104-feet church tower makes, as Nikolaus Pevsner acclaims, 'a group among the happiest in Somerset'. Happy indeed is this perpendicular tower with buttresses and pinnacles, slightly detached from the solid tower, with blank arcading. Happy and assured is the two-storied porch, which has a fan-vaulted ceiling, and the church really rejoices in memorials by some of the country's foremost twentieth-century artists.

Possibly the most visited piece is the statue by Alfred Munnings.

This beautiful equestrian monument of Edward Horner, the last of the family line — who died in 1917 at the age of twenty-three — presently sits on a plinth designed by Edwin Lutyens in the north or Horner chapel, among memorial tablets to other members of the family. We meet Munnings again at Wiveliscombe, in a happier mood and a later war. In this small chapel there is a stained glass window by Sir Charles Nicholson and a cross by Eric Gill. Edwin Lutyens may possibly have designed the First World War memorial in the village, being a friend of the Horners, whose daughter Katherine married Raymond Asquith, who also died in the First World War. In the churchyard the poet and novelist Siegfried Sassoon is also buried. Sassoon, was one of the poets who survived; he returned to write much more, dying in 1967. Ronald Knox, the Catholic preacher, also lived in Mells and said mass in a new chapel where his life is commemorated.

On the wall of the bell tower another local work to see, by Burne-Jones: a stone relief memorial on wood for Laura Lyttelton, surrounded by classical pilasters, which contrast with the curving long tail of a peacock. Another piece in the Pre-Raphaelite style, with angels and beautiful colours in the flowers, is an embroidered work by Mrs Horner, a friend of Edward Burne-Jones.

Among this felicitous, medieval architecture you will discover Meadows Nursery. Behind a long and historically interesting wall in the middle of the village Sue Lees, a Somerset plantswoman who knows and really loves her progeny, has for the last twenty years, cared for the plants she sells; sowing and propagating with great skill. I think of her as the horticultural equivalent of a highly trained Norland Nanny. None of her charges are allowed out before they are strong enough to make their own way into the wider world of our gardens. They are given the best diet — no peat here — and the best support. When ready, they come out, like debutantes, and then Sue tells us how and where they will thrive!

Firstly you walk through her inspiring cottage garden, a

profusion of pink, green and purple in early summer, under the stone arch covered with honeysuckle and roses, to the nursery and main garden.

Sue and her partner Eddie — a garden designer who helps when he has the time — lease this half-acre walled garden from the Earl of Oxford's estate, which still owns much of Mells. Immediately, beyond the north wall — and this is almost the best connective moment — the meadow rises from a dip in ha ha fashion, to the distance. With five superb trees and the River Mells, the garden enjoys an Arcadian vista.

Formerly this was the rectory fruit and vegetable garden — doubtless feeding many — and was tended in the last war by evacuees. Now some of the old lichen-covered apple trees play host to rambling roses, and add structure. To this serene space they have added new beds, bog gardens, delicate grasses, paths and two large ponds, with running water flowing along rills. This has created a Zen or reflective atmosphere that encourages you to sit, and make contact with the landscape.

Sue has planted up the beds with examples of specimens that you can also buy. In spring there are the small pale yellow flowers of epimedium to which she introduced me for my first Somerset garden. They confirm spring's arrival, as does the pink *Dicentra spectabilis* which does so well in Somerset. After rain this gives the same charming droplet effect on its leaves as alchemilla. We have agreed that the peony shoots are perhaps even more glamorous at this first, velvety red stage as they pierce the soil, than later when they bloom. Along the paths are clumps of deep pink *Hellebore orientalis* and the first of the pale blues — *Brunnera macrophlya*, and near the north wall, the scent of an early box in flower.

Many of these plants are for sale, set out in neat rows, and as the seasons progress so new, irresistible perennials and shrubs which have been pampered, are also added.

Nunney: a village with a castle

Just south-west of Frome the small village of Nunney is the proud possessor of the monumental Nunney Castle, to which Pevsner gives the accolade: 'aesthetically the most impressive castle in Somerset'. This was built in the late fourteenth century in the romantic tradition of Scotney in Kent and Bodiam in East Sussex. It is absolutely central to this village. From every angle there is a view that can be seen from most of the houses and gardens, giving the residents, I imagine, great pleasure — and I still relish the frisson, as I approach from Nunney Catch, of seeing the massive towers rising above the village roofs. Perhaps this is one place that might be even better, seen from the hot air balloons that hang in the skies above the Mendips!

Vita Sackville-West described the castle as 'a tiny copy of the Paris Bastille', yet this was originally a manor house. It was crenellated with a licence obtained in 1373 by John de la Mare, sheriff of Somerset and keeper of Old Sarum near Salisbury. The earlier Norman lords were the de Mohuns, who exchanged this manor of Nunney for Dunster. We meet the de Mohuns again at the other end of the county.

This strictly symmetrical, oblong castle follows the patterns of Edward I's mighty castles in North Wales, but if defence had really been the object, then siting it high up on the road to Whatley, where you can see over to the Westbury White Horse, would have been the answer. The castle is at least sixty feet high, and the length of sixty-four feet is almost twice the width of twenty-seven feet. Nunney's particular feature is the concentration of towers: two pairs of angled towers almost meet, with a minimal amount of wall on the shorter sides, from which, in John Collinson, historian and rector of Long Ashton's, day — 1791, trees and shrubs grew 'exhibiting a fine picturesque scene of desolated grandeur!'

It had four storeys: a basement; the kitchen on the ground floor, with evidence of a fireplace large enough for a whole ox; above this the great hall; and then the chapel and solar on the topmost storey. Above this, machicolations or projecting galleries were designed for dropping missiles on marauders — unsuccessfully against Colonel Fairfax in the Civil War.

The historian C.R.B. Barrett includes a delightful sketch of Nunney in his book of 1894. And he also describes a notebook in the British Museum in which he found a 'curious little pen and ink sketch' and notes written by a Royalist, Richard Symonds, who visited in 1644 when the Catholic Prater family held a garrison here for the king. In the sketch, the towers are conical and the roof is not flat, as one might imagine, but high pitched. This led Barrett to question how the castle was defended, as the machicolations

Nunney Castle

were omitted. Subsequently the castle was battered and besieged and had to surrender to Fairfax's troops on 16 September 1645. Evoking the style of his grandfather John Piper who lived nearby, Luke Piper has made a striking painting of the castle.

Seemingly unaffected by all this, the village is clustered about the castle and across from Nunney Brook there lies a tranquil fifteenth-century church within a yew-lined path. The village has several small houses dating from between 1693 and 1744, and larger houses, notably the Manor House, built in true Palladian manner by Sir William Whitchurch, who bought the castle in 1720. These, then, are the elements of a justly conserved area, together with the site of a Roman villa, excavated at Lower Whatley in the nineteenth century, just two miles distant via a pleasant walk beside the river.

But Nunney is far from being mothballed. Village trade and industry, as elsewhere, has declined since the edge tool makers at Mells closed, with naturally fewer shops than in 1883, when there was a milliner along with a shoemaker and several bakers. But Nunney is fortunate in possessing a large village shop near the thatched bus shelter, and a separate post office. One postmaster, who held the reins for thirty-five years, combined his duties with farming, tailoring and drapery as well as holding the position of school clerk and overseer.

For its size Nunney's Street Fair has a large following, and the streets and the castle grounds are filled with stalls, sideshows and music on the first Saturday in August. This event can be traced back to the first charter awarded by Henry III in 1259 for a Wednesday market and a three-day fair. It appears that in 1279 the competition with Frome was not to the liking of the lord of the Frome hundred, who tried to stop it. Much later, on the occasion of the fair's revival in 1959, the village gave the proceeds to the restoration of the cross, originally in the churchyard, which was found in pieces in a builder's yard and reinstated beside the stream.

Where the Parliamentarian forces and cannon slighted the castle and put the Royalist, Colonel Richard Prater, to flight, today, the only noise that breaks the tranquillity, is a natural one, from the ducks diving for crumbs, (on one occasion from this writer's picnic). Now this monumental ruin takes kindly to visitors, and angling, with a permit, and it appears that the crayfish I saw caught by one young lad can be found 'quite often'. In the 1790s the moat was choked with weeds and rubbish, however the above is evidence that it is healthier today.

The following recipe of 1400 for a crayfish, virtually contemporary with the castle's heyday, could be a simpler precedent of a more recent dish of dressed crab or lobster, using oil, mustard and breadcrumbs. But it has to be the right crayfish!: 'A crewes-a dyght him thus-departe hym a sonder, and slyte the belly and take out y fysshe, pare away the reed skynne and mynce it thynne- put vynegre in the dysshe and set on ye table without hete'.

In December the ruins ring with the sound of carols while the walls flicker again with candlelight. Across the brook to All Saints, another Somerset church with Saxon origins. It has a Norman font with a Jacobean circular cover. And although the thirteenth-century chancel arch is much altered, underneath, formerly spanning the south transept, is a section of a fine fifteenth-century oak screen; one of the best examples of such carving in Somerset. This is the

Thatched bus shelter

remains of a rood screen, little seen in this eastern edge of the county. There are two pairs of effigies: one possibly of Sir John Poulet and his wife, who gained his wealth from wool, the other probably Sir Richard Prater and wife. And it has been suggested that the interesting wall painting revealed in 1896, above one of the nave piers, commemorates St George.

The original sixteenth-century wagon roof is awaiting repair, to which all the proceeds from fundraising are directed, whilst the aisle roofs have already been completed. It is apparent that the parishioners of Nunney care deeply for their church and its grounds.

Outside in the churchyard you might, as I did, experience an optical illusion created by the rising ground which, from one point, hides the road; so that one only appears to see water beyond the wall. As a large amount of lime was washed down the stream from the hills, Nunney became a good site for tempering steel and manufacturing edge tools, made for example by Isaac Fussell & Co. Cloth making, weaving, masonry, blacksmithing, dyeing, carding and butchering, along with regular trades, brought considerable wealth, (hence the fine houses), and made for the smooth running of village life. One still might find oneself talking to a retired builder who knows all the older houses that he has worked on here and in Frome.

Another view of the River Mells

In what was the potter, Philip Wood's, beautiful bow-fronted shop, a group of local artists are collaborating in showing their work. For some time Philip made his own particular mark on this village. He has only moved a very short distance to Whatley, where he still produces functional, beautiful pieces: wonderful tea pots, mugs, deep salad bowls, pitchers and jugs — sold nationally and internationally. These are fired in red clay with a contrasting cream slip and then given a soft creamy wash. The colours evoke the soil, and he uses natural forms. Each piece has a different relief of cattle, bees, birds, fish, hares, leaves or maybe a fox, so that the 'sprig' decoration also reminds us of the surrounding environment. Locally a selection of his work is available from the shop at Black Swan Arts.

From inside the bow window, there is another inspiring framed view of the castle and the exterior of the shop melts with great facility into the whole street scene.

Chapter 2

Wells: beauty, antiquity and music

To Axbridge via Cheddar from Wells

*Priddy: the fair, the folk,
the Mendips*

Wells: beauty, antiquity and music

*H*owever many times I see the towers of Wells Cathedral as they come into view around the bend on Dulcote Hill, behind the large trees of the Bishop's Palace, I find myself smiling. Wells Cathedral is the seat of the diocese and the very heart of Somerset. We know changes in the countryside are inevitable but we also know that nothing, absolutely nothing, can alter this magnificent, principally twelfth-century church and its setting. We feel secure.

It is built in local creamy Doulting stone and it has the most beautiful nave; a chapter house that is a composition in fan vaulting, those inimitable worn steps, painted by so many, and the west front is, as Pevsner said, 'the richest receptacle of thirteenth-century sculpture in England'. It is like one vast reredos with nigh on 300 statues that reach the heights where there is a frieze of restored seraphs with six-pointed stone wings.

Winter is my Wells time, when it is most medieval: on a quiet day during Christmas week, when the pomp is over; around Epiphany; or the simple and beautiful ceremony celebrating Bishop Bekynton's death on 14 January 1464. During this evensong, a small posy of flowers and a bowl of water are placed in the chantry commemorating his life, his benefaction to Wells and gift of bringing the water to the city from St Andrew's well in the Palace grounds.

At the end of January, the nave is emptied of chairs and furnishings for a series of promenade concerts, when the audience can walk or stand anywhere in the Cathedral, and sit in the quire stalls. How the organ music of the nineteenth-century French composer Tournemire and the Gregorian chant of two cantors — which filled the whole Cathedral on one occasion — can bring the music and architecture so close, is one of the marvels of this Gothic space.

Perhaps Anthony Trollope's *The Warden* does owe something to Wells, although the author would not name names. Rather, he explains: 'let us presume that Barchester is a quiet town in the West of England, more remarkable for the beauty of its cathedral and the antiquity of its monuments than for its commercial prosperity.' The close at the west end is as it was in Barchester, and paths cross the lawns, where the delightful sight of hundreds of Somerset children folk-dancing graces the green in summer. This green is surrounded by fine houses, including the museum, which was formerly the Chancellor's house. The sumptuous Vicars' Close an enclosed

The west front in winter

planned street of 1348, although altered, presents as one, which no one fails to stop and admire. And through Brown's Gate to Sadler Street and the Swan Hotel. Built in 1497 and one of the oldest in the city, the Georgian panelling, generous fire, seats, cathedral view (deliberately created by the demolition of a house opposite in the 1890s) and a tray of tea preserve the Barchester-ness of Wells.

On Easter Eve, the Cathedral is dark again for the Vigil and the Blessing of the New Fire, with an atmosphere only flickering candlelight, procession and plainsong can bring. For me being part of evensong, held in the oak quire — looking through the ogee arches at the light playing on their crocketed finials, the pointed springing, together with the singing by the choir — is a

34

timeless experience.

Wells and its music are one score. Opposite the north porch, in what was once the thirteenth-century hall of the Archdeanery, the students of Wells Cathedral School give concerts and recitals to the public, when we are treated to tremendous music: an enviable repertoire, playing that transports and worthy of any professional ensemble. Through frequent concerts one is able to follow students through their careers until they leave to study at notable colleges elsewhere. I have heard world premieres, spent a weekend listening to a double-bass fest, (now a regular event), and immersed myself in lyrical concerti and quartets, with the shelves packed with scores. The audience is necessary for their performing skills, however it is the immediacy and intimacy of these concerts — unparalleled, I believe, at other venues — which makes one feel part of music-making.

From the windows of the Chain Gate, which crosses St Andrew's Street, linking the Chapter House with Vicars' Hall of 1348, there is the panorama of the western edge of the city with the small humps of Knowle and Hay Hills in the near distance. From here, there are painterly sunsets; and with one's back to Brown's Gate (built by Bekynton) the west front appears fired heavenly golden by the setting sun.

Wells Museum was founded by Mr Balch in the nineteenth century with his collection of minerals, and grew. It includes samplers, ceramics and natural history; another small Somerset museum run entirely by volunteers and open on Sundays throughout the year and late in the evening through summer.

The charming building is primarily eighteenth century, replacing a fourteenth-century canonical house, with two projecting wings and a splendid run of three Venetian windows on the first floor; these give views of the Cathedral. The collection explains why all early visitors, settlers and colonisers came to the region — the conjunction of water, stone, minerals and the rich pasture derived from all three. A Bronze-Age Beaker with hatched decoration makes us consider the importance of man's simple objects; a delightful Roman hair comb, the everyday of the past; an Iron-Age weaving comb, almost the size of a large foot, made from a deer antler, natural history and man's continuing dependency on the environment. Whilst a carved oak door from one of the Bekynton's fifteenth-century so-called new works — the terrace of houses on the Market Place — illustrates the dignity of craft, and the quality of workmanship funded by wealth and patronage. A small replica, dolls' house size, of Halliday's antique shop, once in the High Street, carved by the founder's grandson, will enthral the children who visit. I find the geological wall map in relief — illustrating all the different hill ranges in the county — fascinating.

The Mendips have safeguarded Wells from sprawl and although the former mills and other industrial buildings are now housing, remarkably, most of Wells is confined to the street plan of the late 1300s. The street pattern is long and narrow, running from east to west, with the proximity to the countryside always apparent.

To see one of these axes, through Brown's Gate again, to Chamberlain Street for a good assortment of windows, doors especially, and the Tuscan-columned entrance of the former Hamilton mansion. Quite a different street in November, for viewing the super-bright, super-noisy, Somerset tradition of carnival as it follows its route along here with its thousands of lights and thunderous music.

Or the other side of the High Street, a parallel east–west axis runs along Silver Street, following the tumbling River Sheppy, past Palace Farm, where the cow-filled yard reminds us of farming. Further west is wide Southover, formerly the main entrance to the city with lanes and courts, that once housed industry, running off. This is one of the best streets in which to visualise the medieval. Behind some of the Georgian and Victorian façades of High and Chamberlain Streets there are still medieval foundations, and many shops still keep their splendid stone fireplaces.

We can get some idea of life in Wells during the reign of Queen Anne through the diary of Dr Claver Morris, a country doctor who had a beautiful house in the Liberty, now part of the Cathedral School. Very much part of the town, he frequented the Crown Coffee House and there read the daily paper. He understood music and was versed in the use of flowers and herbs as medicine. He owned land that supplied the household with bacon, butter and barley meal.

Farming was the backbone of this area and in 1725 Defoe wrote: 'no county in England furnishes more effectual provisions, nor in proportion, a greater value than this', when making his Somerset tour. Although Wells, the city, is thronging with tourists on sunny Saturdays it is still very much dependent on the custom of the outlying villages. Not so long ago I stood in the last feed mill before it closed. Waiting among farmers reminded me that Wells was very much an agricultural centre, a hub for all the satellite villages nearby, such as Wookey Hole.

And of course the farmers came to sell at the markets; these were possibly held in the Market Place before the first charter of 1201. By looking up at the first-floor level of the High Street one can see clues to Wells's eighteenth and nineteenth-century trading history. The city has two open-air markets each week, which include a Wednesday Farmers' Market. Almost always there is a friend to join for coffee. And among the stalls people can dally just as they always did; the Saturday display of fish brings eager queues and you can order in advance. Even the wintry Mendip elements never deter these traders.

You can see a wide range of building styles, from the medieval double jetties of the Crown Hotel, to late nineteenth-century Arts and Crafts revival. One gift shop retains a carved display fascia detail and enchanting narrow walled garden, with a Strawberry Hill Gothic back door. Next the high Gothic revival of Stuckeys Bank (now NatWest), with its carved stone decoration by William Halliday, also a woodcarver, self taught, who lived at

Chilton Polden.

A photograph of the High Street, from the Phillip's collection, in the museum's care, shows, looking towards the Cathedral, earlier shopkeepers and innkeepers and the importance they gave to good hanging signs and entrances: an attitude we should foster today.

Wealth can always be measured in the number of inns and there were many in the High Street. Number 33 was probably one, in brick and materially an odd-man-out in this townscape. But pause longer opposite number 35 for more gracious, larger, first-floor windows — this was the Somerset Hotel until the mid-1870s. The earliest recording of an inn on this site was in 1404. This hotel had an elegant, cast-iron, covered porch giving shelter to arriving guests. It was later occupied, then bought by William Halliday whose work was shown at the Great Exhibition and can still be seen in the city and Cathedral; all five sons inherited his exceptional skills.

There is a Halliday connection with number 58 High Street, which in 1885 was bought by him for his daughter to run a sweetshop. It appears to be the only example of a late nineteenth-century revival of pargetting — decorative plasterwork — in Wells. Did Mr Halliday use as his reference the small example of this medieval style on the front of the exquisite double-jettied house at 7 Sadler Street?

The lanes that lead off High Street — Guardhouse and Mill Lane, which have a small antiques centre with a very helpful and knowledgeable second-hand book dealer — once had mills and here there is a covered street. The courts off Southover and West Street all housed the core of fourteenth-century industry which was tanning, fulling and rack yards, for stretching cloth. Now, this is a quiet backwater, but with a little imagination one can almost smell the processes and hear the sounds of cloth making.

The city had more cloth merchants in 1340 than Coventry,

a reputation which attracted entrepreneurs from the Midlands and France to trade and build their fourteenth-century property portfolios. Medieval women also had important roles, as tapsters and traders, and as landlords in their own right. Marjorie de Moniers was one. Her husband Peter, a merchant from Amiens, was so successful that a lane, now disappeared, was named after him. This ran between Chamberlain and High Street, parallel to Union Street (medieval Grope Lane). For an enchanting legacy of historic shopping look for the small sign in Priest Row where Richard Nichols, a mason, lived with Sarah and sold tea, coffee and snuff. Might this have been an open-fronted shop?

At this point we reach St Cuthbert, which Pevsner calls 'the largest parish church in Somerset, and one of the most interesting', with a roof that takes time to examine. The beams are painted in red, gold and blue and have 'demi' figures of angels centred in the tie beams and fixed to the main beams. It is often mistaken for the Cathedral because it is the first church people meet as they arrive from the west. Surrounding the church are three sets of almshouses, some with their own gardens.

Each Friday, there is another kind of market. Before the doors are opened regulars wait patiently for meringues, pies, home-made bread, chocolate cakes, the best raspberry jam in the county and unsprayed apples with names such as Ellington Pippin. And one can buy some of the best bunches of garden flowers picked that morning by two ladies who both open their respective Mendip gardens for the National Garden Scheme

Wells itself is a place for visiting gardens. In the Close there is one, which is in the process of being revived. This is the former Deanery and once the home of Dean William Turner who wrote *A New Herball,* published between 1551-1568. Over the wall there is an unsurpassed view of the west front. Then passing through both Penniless Porch and the Bishop's Eye across the drawbridge and through the Gatehouse, one finds the gardens of the Bishop's Palace. Cedars with wide, low branches brush velvet lawns beyond the ruins of the thirteenth-century Great Hall. A pilgrim cast in bronze stands on the south lawn.

At the south-eastern corner of the rampart wall, past a large sculpture of Adam and Eve, the path leads to the inner moat walk. Over the bridge is the Well House, views of the Palace and Cathedral, and the Jubilee Arboretum. Curving flowerbeds surround the water. The Bishop's Palace, which celebrates its 800th anniversary in 2006, is in this setting, 'without doubt the most memorable of all bishops palaces in England'. Some of its sumptuous ceilings, panelling and art are shown to visitors in the entrance hall, the long gallery and drawing room. Tea and lunch can be taken as you look out over these lawns and trees or in the undercroft of the Palace.

Walking up New Street to the foot of Bristol Road brings one to some large wrought-iron gates, which lead to an eighteenth-century landscape garden, Walcombe. Locally known as the 'Combe', it is generously opened by the Tudway

The Vale of Avalon from Milton Lodge Gardens

Quilter family. No traffic jars the peace of this tree-filled grove, where children can relax and where imagination can take over. Travel on up the steep lane — the Old Bristol Road — to Mr and Mrs Tudway Quilter's own garden – Milton Lodge. Looking out from the beautifully-managed terraces in front of the eighteenth-century house, Somerset fills the horizon. The panorama is pastoral: it could well be a Constable landscape — sheep graze below, with the Cathedral, Palace, woods and the Vale of Avalon beyond. Sometimes garden teas are served at the stable block. This combination of intimate corners, spacious lawns and vistas will always come to mind when I see, in my own garden, the long-blooming hot pink flowers of the autumn aster, 'Alma Pötschke', of which they gave me a cutting. And the hornbeam which was going to outgrow my last garden, which the Milton Lodge gardeners carefully transported to the lower field of the estate, is I am told, thriving!

To Axbridge via Cheddar from Wells

When I first saw the Somerset sunsets, they were a complete revelation. To catch more I sometimes drove a few miles from Wells towards Axbridge with the Mendip range in the north-west — I could chase the last of these exquisite rays. As I got to know this road better, I found other reasons to pause and a bus does the whole journey.

Rodney Stoke is one village on this route that has become an obligatory stop, especially in the asparagus season when bunches are available from a farm off the lane leading to the parish church — there is usually a sign on the road. You may be lucky enough to catch these green bundles of pure spring during the six cutting weeks from around mid-April to the end of May. If the asparagus is over, a small table outside another farm often has an offering: maybe a jug of anemones, spring onions or broad beans. Opposite the church there is an unusual three-storied farmhouse just off the road across the moors back to Wedmore and Glastonbury.

Having passed the fields and selling huts for strawberries — some of the last left in England, there is Cheddar, where on a Tuesday a country market takes place in the hall opposite the parish church with its 110-feet spire. The parish rooms are also the venue for a Farmers' Market.

As Cheddar developed over the last 150 years, so visitors arrived by rail and through the opportunities afforded by charabanc tours, which brought tourists after the First World War. But earlier, in 1869, the Cheddar Valley Line was built —

one of three before 1878 that stopped at Wells — now there are none! This also gave visitors from Bristol and the Midlands the chance to visit the famous caves, cliffs or gorge. To serve the car-driving excursionists — the Cave Man Café, designed by G.A. Jellicoe and Russell Page — was opened in 1933, one of the first modernist buildings in Somerset.

With all this Cheddar has acquired a sort of seaside feel. The town grew westwards from the market cross, so that charming 1920s bungalows became part of the scene; Cheddar has a mixture of older Victorian villas and some picturesque nineteenth-century houses. These are quite separate from the gorge; around the streets you can still find market gardeners who have been here sixty years and more, growing strawberries in their gardens and selling them at the gates, but not any longer in chip baskets. The baskets were an industry of their own; made of woven chestnut, rarely seen now, except in a museum.

A recently restored 1920's cheese emporium at Cheddar

However just a mile or two up beyond the gorge, for those who seek it, there is still utter peace and beauty. A friend and I found it so, as we walked through Long Wood in early May when the sea of bluebells and wild garlic is a haze among the broad-leaved trees. Near the stone walls lambs were grazing and we saw early purple orchids. It was on these cliffs that William Maton, making his observations around 1794, noted the famous Cheddar pink — *Dianthus coefius* — only found on the Cheddar cliffs in July, distinguished by its single flower.

The road curves around the Cheddar reservoir and so reaches small, medieval Axbridge, a royal manor and a town with its own Latin Chronicle, compiled in the fourteenth century. It is the best example of a hill-juxta-moor town in our region. It lies at the foot of the Mendip range where the hills run down to the fertile strawberry-growing moors and was once the hunting ground of Saxon Kings from Æthelstan to St Edward.

The air hereabouts has been described as 'soft and salubrious' and Maton felt that 'Mendip may be called the *Alps* of Somersetshire as the peak may be of Derbyshire'. Whilst Alan Tarbat, a former master of the Junior School at Wells Cathedral School — who wrote charmingly about Somerset just after the Second World War, in the age of the train — began his Axbridge article thus: 'To-day I am going to take you to Switzerland, get your purse and take a railway ticket for Axbridge, for it must be the rail that takes you to Switzerland'. It closed in 1963. He promised that his readers would 'gasp in wonder at the loveliest little lake' (reservoir) and 'the ringing of its delectable mountains' — being the Mendips, and knolls.

Doubtless Tarbat had the gable ends and half timbering of King John's Hunting Lodge in his mind's eye. But this description has a resonance today. Even by car, especially now that Axbridge is bypassed, there is a sense of having arrived somewhere else. The town is snugly enclosed by Shute Shelve Hill, sheltered from the north and north-west. With the tall medieval buildings on three sides, as one sits in the Square — even with the weakest rays of sun — one gets a continental sun-trap experience.

Elsewhere Axbridge is described as a handsome, small town of great antiquity. The town was initially shaped by these hills but was further fashioned by King Alfred, who established one of his three *burhs,* or fortified camps, here as defence against the Danes, when he was hiding in the Isle of Athelney.

Axbridge was granted several charters over 400 years: the first given by King John, followed by Henry III. The town was incorporated into a borough with a charter granted by Philip and Mary in 1556 and was awarded yet another by Elizabeth I in 1599 to provide for two more fairs, making it four. You can see the original documents and seals in the Somerset Record Office. The rich evidence of the houses in the High Street and the memorials in the church reveal that a good deal of wool trading must have taken place in the mid-to-late seventeenth century. But it was through the reclaiming of the moor in the late eighteenth century that Axbridge gained its agricultural prosperity, so that in the nineteenth century with the advent of the railway, crops of peas, potatoes and strawberries, thriving here still, could be speedily distributed to Birmingham, Bristol and London.

First one should make for the Square and the superb timber-framed King John's Hunting Lodge, belonging to the National Trust and restored to its former glory in 1971.

It is now a museum, managed by an independent trust that displays geological finds, evidence of two Roman villas and the history you might need for a town walk. The Lodge was built in the late 1400s but not for the King: he would have hunted the Mendip Forest around 1200. This is a built exemplar of the period, a material microcosm of the once-rich civic and social life of the town. The intricate construction, with notably the dragon beam and posts, is explained and ongoing exhibitions cover the town's importance and its built development.

Three merchant's shops once occupied the ground floor that may have opened onto the street, with working and sleeping floors above. What did they sell? The original stairs are carved around one single newel post — a feat of great carpentry, but a chink in the panelling gives sight of the earlier reed and plaster construction. And then on the upper floor a fine, ogee-headed window with quatrefoils in spandrels shows the Mendip hills running towards the east. But be warned, the wide planks in these rooms and the staircase tend to have a sloping will of their own!

In the High Street and, unbelievably through today's eyes, the former main road, there is a carved late fifteenth-century door of exceptional width that won an accolade from John Betjeman, as the best butcher's shop door in the country. This was one of many butchers' shops in Axbridge — another outward sign of wealth and trade. However like so many of the former shops, this is converted, yet one hopes that the decorative tiles and door will become part of the conversion. Next the Manor House with another magnificent door and slated cupola, then St Jude's, a smaller timber-framed house which has had many lives. Along the length of the High Street house-proud owners paint up their front doors in blue and white and green. For sale, outside one house is a tiny table with marrows and cucumbers in August, and simple jam jars of flowers on the window ledge.

Like so many Somerset churches, St John Baptist, which has a fine position overlooking the Square, provides several surprises — a sensitive restoration being one. After an archaeological survey carried out around 1870, it was considered that the state of the 600-year-old church had become pitiable.

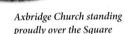

45

Axbridge Church standing proudly over the Square

John Dando Sedding was a leading ecclesiastical architect and produced work in several styles; a pupil of G.E. Street, who extracted the essence of this conglomerate and Doulting stone church with the hand of one very closely involved with the Arts and Crafts movement.

His work has mercifully not detracted from the glorious 1636 nave ceiling with its raised plasterwork, from the delicate fan vaulting in the crossing tower, nor from the original, painted north aisle ceiling, where there is still an image of a green man. He added (or replaced) a part close screen, in Art Nouveau style with beautiful lettering and 'remarkable details', and created his own pattern design for the palely, tinted glass windows.

The church is full of colour, in particular the fine baroque decoration surrounding Ann Prowse's memorial in the Lady Chapel. This memorial has an astonishing framing of half angels and half mermaids. There are more colours in the interesting, pictorial needlework, representing how the communion table was organised, by Mrs Prowse, daughter of the Bishop of Wells, which took seven years to complete.

On one late August morning my view from the curving church steps, of a stall-filled Square, might not have been so very different from one those earlier merchants would be familiar with, for a combined market and fair was unmarred by traffic when the streets were closed. Produce stalls sold beef, dairy products and lamb from local farms, and there were enough strawberries for all. On the other hand the fresh cake and pie stalls made a poignant contrast with the baked contents of a cabinet in the church named 'Spearing's gift'; a donation first made in 1690 being 'four shillings per week in bread to be given to the second poor' — those not poor enough to be on the parish — and given in perpetuity.

A delightful door

Like so many other Somerset towns or villages Axbridge was completely self-sufficient; with a seed merchant and a saddler, collar and harness-maker who advertised his 'fittings and requisitions at Bristol prices'. There were a handful of dressmakers and coach builders — Axbridge wanted to keep up with the current style, however a tourist guide of 1885 plugged this as an 'old fashioned spot, which not even the iron horse can rouse into life'.

Alongside the church I took a rising path above the town roofs and large gardens, from where I could see Glastonbury Tor, and the vast tract of reclaimed moor, for market gardening. After making these excursions, I asked a very dear friend Chlöe West, who spent her childhood in Axbridge, for her 1950s memories. She recalled taking this path up to the station, when the 'iron horses still ran'. Here Mr Lush the stationmaster, an imposing and bewhiskered figure with a watch chain, bred angora rabbits. And then she remembered more, and a lovely picture emerged of the nature walks which her headmaster arranged in the summer, when the children would walk out from school, straight onto the moor. In late May from my seat in the Square I could hear the reassuring sound of children playing in the school playground at lunchtime. Long may these voices be heard in Somerset! There is a danger that as a town — even one that has attracted tourists for many years — becomes more gentrified and holiday homes proliferate, it becomes mothballed, loses its amenities or heaven forbid, its school.

Priddy: the fair, the folk, the Mendips

Take your pick through either of the dramatic Cheddar or Ebbor gorges, to bring you on top to Priddy where a matter-of-fact 'wildishness' characterises the village. Despite this, a deep-rooted community spirit flourishes between the scattered farmsteads of the large parish, and those that live around the green share a common relationship with it.

This is an ancient settlement, lying slightly lower and marginally more sheltered than the nearby North Hill, although 'on Mendip' means weather. Priddy has a singular Somerset-ness in its unchanging links with the land. It is among, surrounded by and riddled with stone circles, long barrows, tumuli and caverns. Once a Roman road ran from Green Ore to Charterhouse, where there was a Roman fortlet, whilst the River Axe springs from the Mendips in Swilden's Hole, next door to Manor Farm on the lower green. It then travels underground to Wookey Hole whose course cavers have followed.

My Priddy memories are many-imaged: the journey, the terrain itself, the inns, the fairs, the wildlife walks and dancing at the village hall. What was the former Bristol road passes the red door of Walcombe and Milton Lodge and as you climb the winding hill there is a commanding view south over Wookey Hole and to the west as far as Brent Knoll — worth stopping for.

At the top, at a crossroads, you encounter an unprepossessing building with granite-coloured render and a faded hand-painted wooden sign. Looking for all its worth as though it never opens, it could well be an understudy for Jamaica Inn. In fact, the reputation of the Hunters Lodge Inn is not unsung or unappreciated: in truth it is an important slice of old Mendip. I was first introduced to this idiosyncratic pub by a local and I recollect that it was also a welcome finale to an evening with Somerset Wildlife Trust members to hear nightjars — nocturnal as their name implies. The scrub and gorse that has been allowed to grow back is a habitat that encourages these migrants. Around 10 pm, just as it is getting dark between June and September, they can be heard roosting, making their churring noise; when they take off it is more of a whoop and sounds as ancient as the barrows and tumuli on North Hill.

Early man started digging here for lead, long before the Romans whose main mine was at Charterhouse. Until the beginning of the last century the mines provided work for many local people — hence one of the four pubs being named the Miners Arms. It is now a house, but I remember it having an unequalled reputation in the 1960s for good food and snails!

From the Hunters Lodge Inn you can walk straight into the landscape, now a nature reserve and a Site of Special Scientific Interest (SSSI). Once this would have echoed with the sound of flint, noisy and indeed polluting. Now the ivy-covered ruins, the hussock-covered craters, humps, pools which freeze in winter and the broken chimneys are the detritus of Victorian smelter workings; the only evidence in this 'gruffy ground'. But the workings were halted in 1908 when lead pollution became a hazard in the Axe stream flowing down to Wookey Hole.

In that same year at Charterhouse W.D. Caröe converted what had originally been a social centre for miners into a delightful small church called St Hugh's. Jennifer Freeman in her biography describes it 'Perhaps Caröe's most romantic accomplishment in church work resides in this little building'. High up on the Mendips with its rough-cast and rendered 'dying' buttresses it has a 'Voysey-ish' air. Charles F. Annesley Voysey was an architect who sought to make a connection between his houses and their setting. Somerset was a perfect location for him to demonstrate this ethos, using vernacular forms and local materials which we shall meet in west Somerset. Like Tivington church, also in west Somerset, this too has a fireplace, once part of the social centre. The work by Caröe — a revered Arts and Crafts architect, for churches and cathedrals all over the country, forms a catalogue that glitters with commissions from Durham and St David's Cathedral to

Climb and walk on Mendip

many in this county. This conversion, completed in 1930, took just over twenty years because it was, evidently, carried out by the miners themselves.

The Mendip Hills gave up another, even more precious, metal to those who were prepared to work for it. We do not have to look far to see the result of its use in the elegant brass chandeliers at Wedmore and Axbridge parish churches. Calamine was an important ingredient used in the process of brass founding. It was mined at Shipham and Rowberrow near Black Down, the highest point on Mendip at 1,068 feet (325 metres). All mining ceased with foreign competition, but for many years in the sixteenth and seventeenth centuries it coexisted with farming.

The Hunters is still the cavers' pub. Chances are that there will always be someone who has either just been down or is about to go down the 'hole'. But it is also a local for locals who live in the far-flung parts of the parish, attracting any who appreciate the real inn character. Anyone who arrives here in a downbeat mood will be certain to leave cheered. Company is always to be enjoyed and the Sunday lunch is the same as weekdays: fuelling food before or after a walk. And those seeking imported glamour will not find it: this is grub and beer.

No danger of makeover here — seventy years unaltered. It has a central panoptical three-sided bar counter from which the landlord and his wife can see and serve three rooms. Beer is from the barrel and includes local Butcombe. Inside is dark by default, not design. There is a fire, simple tables, a very old hearth, now containing a high-backed settle, chairs that have been there since the war and little decoration other than the genuine fire pieces and the odd village photo. Pewter tankards hang above the bar for their owners, known by name. This is the sort of inn where 'if it isn't broke it won't be fixed'.

Food is always the same: a plate of energy such as pasties or faggots and peas. Bread and cheese comes cavers' size and the ham rolls have a real filling of ham. What takes place here has taken place in country pubs for centuries, usually begun by a farmer as a sideline, possibly selling the beer or cider he made in the cider house from the apples grown in his own orchard. The warmth and sociability are all the more cherished because of its isolation. No coffee or tea here, but for this writer and scores of other visitors it has been the inn where 'once in' you are known by name or pursuit. Here, uninhibited, anyone can put the world to rights.

Walking to or ambling around or off from the village green is a pleasure in itself. Another lane north leads to a view of high drama from the edge of the Mendips — with Somerset stretching away before your eyes as far as the Quantock Hills. Just further along the Cheddar road, the last farm in the village, Townsend, has just started to sell the meat from the cattle they breed and rear up here, at a tiny shop. You can also sample it at the Victoria Inn, which has two good fires. Making the third is the New Inn right on the lower green, once indeed a farmhouse about 130 years ago.

Depending on your inclination, the Priddy calendar has a choice of more happenings than any other I know of this size. In June Priddy locals dress up their gardens and open them to all comers on a Sunday, with a trail and, importantly, an excellent home-made tea served in the village hall. It is a chance to walk, meet the residents and see horticultural variations, from small cottages to the Victorian Rectory, often with more unexpected views.

The July Priddy Folk Festival, coming of age in 2006, attracts acts from all over the world. We just caught the final notes and tent dismantling last year; a brilliant summer Sunday when many were reluctant to leave and jamming continued spontaneously in the pub gardens. Next, held at Fern Hill Farm, is the Big Green Gathering, an environmental jamboree for all ages, including everything from solar-powered cinema to permaculture: from sustainable living to healing, with of course, food and farming underpinning the whole.

Judging by the recent parish plan, it would seem that although the parishioners value Priddy in different ways, they arrived at the same conclusion. Priddy is a working village where residents are principally farmers; some work in the quarries and some in the city. Priddy's isolation has an 'incomparable loveliness'. It is the only village with a parish church, between Chewton Mendip and Shipham in the west. However for a week or so in August the quiet hills, the pubs, village hall and twelfth-century church become the setting for equine dealing and sheep selling. I was at the Priddy Sheep Fair within three weeks of moving to Somerset. And on the Sunday evening before the show at the New Inn on the village green, there was an impromptu pony and trap race between the travellers, not necessarily popular with everyone, but none the less exciting.

One needs to visit the show at least once, although it is changing by the year. Recently the horse sales have been separated from the sheep auction with the rows of boxes and horses in another field. It is held year after year on the third Wednesday in August — 2006 being the 656th Priddy Fair. Moving the annual Mendip Sheep Fair, up and away from the City of Wells, is thought to have been done to avoid danger from the spread of the Black Death and since 1348 it has taken place near a landmark on the Green — the thatched hurdle. This selling fair has its own atmosphere, which has evolved, now with the combination of the sheep auction, horses and side stalls.

Later in September, there is another Somerset tradition when the Mendip Ploughing Society holds its matches at Chancellor's Farm. To see the old red-painted, so-called lease lend tractors — they came over from the USA at the end of the war — ploughing the perfect furrow in one direction and a pair of shires pulling the ploughshare in the opposite direction, makes a working canvas of deep red lines. To see the old, and now being revived, skills of stone walling and hedge-laying in competition; to share a table in the farmers' tent, to eat a plate of bread and cheese or ham, with the rain dripping outside, is part of Mendip magic. And leaving, invariably with the rain soaked through my hat and mack, my boots heavy with red clods of mud, makes this a Mendip rite of passage.

Ploughing match on the Mendips

Chapter 3

Somerset rural life: cheese, cider and shows

Bruton: an enigmatic town

Castle Cary, Ansford and more villages

Illustration on previous page: The Bruton Bridges

Somerset rural life:
cheese, cider and shows

'Somersetshire is a land of lush zummer … pasture with a historic lineage and lead in the taste of contents in goodness, with any cheese in England.' One cannot but agree with John Houghton, who wrote this in 1695.

Most will know what is now called 'the Bath and West', the large four-day show organised by the Royal Bath and West of England Society founded in 1777. One active member and local farmer John Billingsly, who lived on the Mendips near Shepton Mallet, was a 'pioneer' in the movement to improve agriculture. It was to counteract the poor returns that cottagers and commoners were getting from their land at that time that he advocated, among many, ideas of enclosure, the drainage of ditches and soil improvement. The society held their first show or rather 'exhibition of fat sheep' in the courtyard of Hetling House in Bath in 1790. From this small beginning the great society grew. It acquired royal patronage in 1809, and travelled to grounds across the whole country as an ambassador for farming in the west. Since 1965 the large site just outside Shepton has been the permanent home for the show and headquarters.

Billingsly's ideas filtered down, and around seventy years later other farmers began to set up their own informal groups, just before mechanisation, whilst the depression of the 1870s and cheaper food imports were not far away. Not far either from where the Royal Bath and West hold their show, a meeting of what was to become the Mid Somerset Agricultural Society was held at Evercreech around the mid-1850s. It may well have begun as an informal forum for farmers who could meet, share ideas, sometimes compete and demonstrate their skills. Some years later, in 1902, the society transferred what had become a show, to its present site in Shepton. As we have grown further from the land, so farmers realise there is a greater need to reconnect the consumer with growing, rearing animals, real food and country callings.

On a Sunday in August, this society will hold its 154th one-day show in a large field in the town to which everyone in the neighbourhood is drawn. Those who farm will want to show their crops and beasts; beekeepers will bring honey and encourage children to taste; cheesemakers hope for a red rosette; hay and silage will be back again in the fodder tent, one of the best for sweet smelling feed. There is healthy competition among the amateur cider makers whilst the Hecks family of Street, professional farm cider makers for 160 years dispense glasses for the strong headed. Country people — including children, who have their own category – who still bake, preserve, sew, make lace, crochet, quilt and grow vegetables can enter the various sections, be it the art and craft or produce and flower tents. As W.R. Lethaby wrote in 1923, pleading this cause: 'Country things have a character and beauty specially their own'. The beauty is here in the country arts, once part of everyday life, before shop cakes, jam and machine embroidery took precedent; a country posy in a jam jar brings you closer to a cottage garden than a bunch of imported 'garage flowers'. Bottles of apple, grape and blackberry wine, treacle tarts, sliced to reveal their juicy filling, sausage rolls, scotch eggs and scones, are all staged 'in one place' and become richer with a good helping of local dialect.

In the main ring there are heavy horses and hunters, dressage, carriage driving and pony carts. Less so now because of the 2001 foot and mouth outbreak, but there are still enough pens of Suffolk sheep, long-haired Lincolns, Dorset Horns, rare breeds, and working Jersey cows — like a supreme champion from the Wadham's herd at Holton whose cream is so Somerset. These classes, judged by the experts wearing bowler hats and white coats, help us to appreciate the skills and the fraternity of farming.

Classic cars get their summer airing, chrome and leather are polished and picnic baskets are the order of the day. Cheese is one of the very best components for picnics, parties and to give as a present. We are more than fortunate to live in what I call 'dairy land'. Under ten miles in any direction, I have access to farms which make some of the best cheese in the world. Strong words, sometimes strong cheese, but between each maker there are subtle and mysterious nuances of taste, which cannot be too easily explained. It is all in the soil, in the composition of ley — the mix of grasses and legumes for summer pasture and winter feed and the starter culture. The art of cheesemaking is a craft combined with science that has to be learnt well.

Taking a southerly direction from Shepton, cheese lovers could make a wheel (not always round I add) of a cheese journey, to locate some of the makers, large and artisan, and buy cheese in assorted shapes and sizes from the farms which have their own shops. However the majority of the following cheeses are sold in good local food shops or at the Farmers' Markets in Wells, Glastonbury or Frome.

The nearest is one of the newcomers. At Wootton Farm, North Wootton the Bartlett brothers make three elegant sheep's cheeses from organic milk; thankfully the number of these specialist makers has recently increased, although this predates cheese made from cow's milk, by centuries.

South-east, on the way to Bruton at Wyke Champflower, Wyke Farms, one of the biggest independent producers in the country, sells among others their extra mature vintage cheddar with a bite and their own butter. Just east at Westcombe unpasteurised Cheddar and Red Leicester-style wheels are made and sold at the Westcombe Farm shop. Chris Duckett, who used to make Caerphilly at Wedmore, has joined them, making his own cheese from the Westcombe milk. A turn south to Keen's, at Moorhayes

Farm, Wincanton for an unusual sixteenth-century farmhouse with a turreted external stair where traditional, prize-winning, farmhouse Cheddar has been made for over 100 years. Keen's are the third member of the slow cheese presidia to which both Westcombe and Montgomery belong. I used to buy this delicious cheese in London over many years for my own café, and still do in Somerset, either from the farm or from the Wincanton country market on a Friday.

Next, north and slightly west to reach North Cadbury, a village to stop in, for the collegiate church and one of the most elegant of village shops which supports Montgomery, the village-made cheese. This is superb, made like the other two with unpasteurised milk. A few years ago I was invited to America to give a lecture on my 'Northern Journey' and cooked a dinner party for my host. And living in Somerset I felt this had to be reflected in the food. So I went in search of lamb and some English cheese to put on the willow cheese tray

A rare sight - milking on the moors near Glastonbury

Sophie Courtiour of Rodney Stoke had made for me to give to my friend. But imagine my delight on finding Montgomery's cheese sold in an excellent food store just outside Washington D.C.!

Back across via Cary, the next stop is Ditcheat where the Barber family at Maryland Farm, one of the oldest in Somerset, have made cheese since 1833. The farm shop sells cheeses and butter and they have launched a cheese to celebrate the farm's long history.

In the last century they made Caerphilly, which was sent to South Wales for the miners to eat, as they found it had good

underground keeping qualities. Possibly more fascinating is the fact that Barber's have taken on the collection of historical starter cultures, or good bacteria, which determines the taste. They supply the key starter to most of the artisan cheesemakers 'grown' from 'mother cultures' that can be traced back to those used in the county for years, giving the indigenous flavour. The farm has more above-the-ground links with the racing stables of Paul Nicholls, fervently supported in the village as the old stabling of Barber's Manor Farm are let and used by the horses being trained here; one much applauded local winner was the 1999 Cheltenham Gold Cup winner — Seemore Business.

Hardly a canter across the Fosse to the beautiful Mendip village of East Pennard where Fred Gould makes a fine cheese, sold in local shops, nationally and from their farm shop, with the rare bonus of a fifteenth-century thatched farmhouse the other side of the yard. They are prizewinners at the Bath and West, the Frome Cheese Show and the Shepton Show.

But if I may divert further, try to make a point of turning up the drove that leads to the Avalon Vineyard and orchards. Twenty-five years ago Hugo Tripp and his wife planted their first vines and have since added a whole range of fruit wines to their organic range; from elderberry to gooseberry and from plum to raspberrry. Together with cider you can buy the whole selection here and pick, as I love to do, the very last of the Autumn Bliss raspberries which capture the intensity of late summer. I like to distil this by making some rapsberry cordial or vinegar to add to winter salads.

At Baltonsborough the Clapp family, who own Brue Valley Farms, have a large dairy, where they too make Cheddar and butter, sold nationally and of course to the Baltonsborough and Butleigh village shops and from their own farm. The last cheesemaker, but not the last slice in the journey, is H.G. Green of West Pennard, who are famous for the large cheese they sent up for Queen Victoria's wedding in 1840. Its flavour didn't find favour on that occasion, as it was unfortunately not eaten for some time, but Green's are now equally well known for their organic Cheddar made with unpasteurised milk from their Swiss brown or brown cross cows. It is available at Hecks Cider Farm Shop in Street.

At the Somerset Rural Life Museum in Glastonbury housed in the Victorian building of the Abbey Farm, a café has been opened in the old cheese room. This farm was owned by the Mapstone family until 1969. But the stone and timber agricultural temple — the nearby Abbey Barn — is of course much older and dates from around the 1340s. This thirty-three feet storehouse for all the Abbey's provisions stood within what would have been their farm, and has a cruck-formed roof that is a marvel.

Naturally the café serves cheese, and both this and the butter are from Clapps; the juice is from Hecks at Street, who have some orchards on the slopes of the Tor; and bread from the Glastonbury bakers, Burns. And you can take your choice of slices, rock cakes, fruit cake and sponges made by friendly volunteers who have run this café for some years.

The museum was opened in 1976 and has displays relevant to the seasons, with a wide range of farming activities from planting and harvesting to animal husbandry. The former cowsheds explain, for example, how peat was stored, in a beehive-like structure, allowing air to circulate between the ruckles. Being in cider country, you can see the method of preparing the 'cheese' — or pomace – the macerated apples, which are layered with straw before being pressed.

140-year-old cider press

I once joined in the real thing, making cider with Keith and Pam

Johnson of Bleadney near Wells in their 140-year-old press — using the method which has been followed for hundreds of years. Those first few drops of apple juice are powerful and have an indescribable taste. The juice only begins to work and ferment when it is in the barrel. If it is a dry season, as it was that particular November, spreading the 'cheese' leaves you with orange-brown stained hands, and I am sure I left a trail of apple-ness as I went about shopping in Wells that morning!

To round off or start the next growing year, there is wassailing, celebrated in January, which the Johnsons organised on their smallholding. Guns are fired through the trees to ward off any evil spirits, cider is poured around the roots of a chosen tree and a piece of toast soaked in the cider is offered. The whole idea is to 'urge' the tree, treated as a living being, to grow better in the next year, all accompanied by the wassail song. Their large bonfire generated much-needed heat on a bitterly cold night, whilst the warm food and live music kept us on our toes and fuelled.

It will be 100 not out at Baltonsborough this year, whose engaging August bank holiday show is gearing towards country crafts and pursuits — with stick carving and hurdle weaving, we hope. This began as a horticultural show. Cider is made on the spot, sheep are sheared and the crafts tent is well supported. One category in last year's cake-making competition caused quite a stir with all the would-be gentleman bakers of the village, for weeks beforehand. As I shop regularly at the village shop, I was able to see the buzz in the weeks running up to the show. There was such a run on some ingredients for the Victoria sponge cake class, that these had to be restricted — presumably for trial baking — for which sandwich tins were also in short supply. All good fun!

Bruton: an enigmatic town

The villages around Bruton also play their part in the great cheese hunt but the town itself offers a quest of a different nature, a worthy and far-reaching history. Local archaeologists and historians are slowly revealing more as they discover the rich and puzzling layers.

What you see in Bruton is only a fraction of what there is, as travellers are obliged to take the one-way system along narrow streets. Much of its architecture is the legacy of patronage and scholarship, which the approach from the south-east hints, as the road passes some of the ancient buildings of King's School. Bruton is a large centre of education: there are not only four schools, but it also has good communication via the railway from Bristol to Dorchester. You can take any one of six different approaches to this one-time thriving market town, where, as William Maton noticed in 1797, 'the vales are meadows, the declivities orchards and the eminences sheep-walks'. This is still so as the town has created its existence along and around the River Brue. For Bruton is surrounded by voluptuous pasture, albeit with seasonal character changes.

To journey down the lanes from Shepton between the undulating Coombe and Creech Hills, that cradle the town, can in winter be an icy and Arthurian experience — Bruton's history of severe floods and snow is well documented, and shown at the museum. But taking a walk in late spring above Providence Place among lanes pervaded by the smell of wild garlic beyond wild flower meadows, the scene glistens. Bruton has a never-ending number of lanes; one is by Mill Dam and upwards to Tolbury Lane, where I passed the duck pond, and found myself sharing a view of the watery wildlife with a young Brutonian.

Some of the first evidence of historical settlement is Romano-British; a Roman temple was discovered at Creech Hill and a tessellated pavement at Discove in 1791. The Saxon King, Ine, and St Aldhelm caused the first church to be built around AD 690 and the buttressed walls, west of the church, were part of the Augustinian priory founded in 1142 by the de Mohuns, who owned estates at Minehead and Dunster. This brings home the scale of their colonisation, from east Somerset to the furthest points of the county. And located high on the southern skyline by the Pillow Mound, beautifully framed when you look out from the museum, is the Dovecote, which surely had an earlier life, perhaps even as a look-out, as John Bishton of the civic society and I have pondered. This landmark of around 1519, one of the National Trust's earliest acquisitions, in some respects chronicles the transition from Priory to Abbey in the period before the dissolution.

The Tudor recorder Leland, journeying slightly later, remarked that 'Brewton was much occupied with the making of clothe', however its first fulling mill was recorded as early as 1129. And it is after him that the trail is named that travels through the town, starting near King Alfred's tower in the east on its way to Castle Cary.

Right on the southerly axis, in a perfect position by the river crossing, is St Mary — one of the 'proudest' churches in Somerset, an elegant fourteenth-century parish church, on a much older site and one of the few that is closely linked to a former monastery. St Mary has two towers: the fifteenth-century west or bell tower, some 102 feet high, and the older, north porch tower, built 100 years earlier. Bruton's occupation with cloth is reflected in the rich additions and embellishments such as a wide sixteenth-century clerestory and timbered nave roof; some seventeenth-century oak carving on the base of the pulpit; and a Jacobean carved inner entrance porch. From earlier periods there is a rare Norman font with small carved columns, (reminding one, in miniature, of the monumental columns at Durham Cathedral); a magnificent thirteenth-century oak chest carved from one single plank; and a fourteenth-century crypt.

In the church, as in the façades of the many 'Georgianised' houses, all is not as it at first seems: only recently has it been confirmed that the puzzling addition of the gilded chancel in the style of the 1740s was actually made in the 1770s by Moulton of Salisbury; revealed by Richard Carpenter — who designed the famous Lancing College chapel – when he worked here in 1868. Near the altar a memorial commemorates the life of Sir Maurice Berkeley and his two wives, once a standard bearer to Henry VIII, who bought Bruton Abbey in the same year as the dissolution.

Autumn bounty on the road from Redlynch

His house stood in Abbey Fields beyond the church and one of his descendants was later made a baron after supporting the Royalist cause. With the wealth the family accumulated through this loyalty they built Berkeley Square, the original Berkeley House, becoming the first developers of Mayfair which of course includes Bruton Street, all in London. Concerts are often held in the church and ongoing research will continue to uncover much more as the stone, the churchyard, walls and memorials are carefully recorded.

Bruton has two bridges and the ancient stepping-stones

linking the town to the school afford one of the best viewing points up-river, where in the right light there is a mirror image of the arched Packhorse Bridge. Here begins a charming walk along Lower Backway. This well-hidden byway, where the Packhorse Fair is held at the end of May, follows the River Brue, which separates the church and King's School, from the town. King's was founded in 1519 by Bishop Fitzjames of London, who was born at nearby Redlynch. From here you can see the gardens and the chapel belonging to yet another institution, which is part of Bruton's living history.

A hanging sign, in the narrow, western end of the High Street takes one through an arch to Hugh Sexey's Hospital, where time is of another age. The hospital was established in 1638 with the proceeds of the estates of Hugh Sexey, one of seven 'auditors to the exchequer' to Elizabeth and James I, and a successful property dealer. Married twice, he died childless and endowed

The growing garden at Sexey's Hospital

this hospital so that twelve residents and originally twelve boys could live here. Each boy was given a new suit of blue clothes every year and 'overseers or visitors' were appointed to ensure his original wishes were maintained. The present-day trustees continue to meet in the visitor's room.

His other wish, that the residents should be provided with a plot of garden so that they could grow the food that they needed, also continues. Although the plots were altered to a Victorian, walled garden of fruit and flowers, today the rows of vegetables, asparagus bed, canes of raspberries and earthed up potatoes —

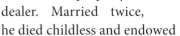

65

grown and well-tended by a gardener, together with those who can help — provide for the residents. Fit and healthy they must be, for even on a bleak winter day there was still a large basket of potatoes to help a stew along!

These gardens and the Georgian gazebo, where I wanted to sit and drink tea, are where residents can enjoy the view of the Dovecote. This can just be glimpsed as you walk to the small chapel, just large enough for the original residents. This and the adjacent hall are open and morning prayer is said daily for anyone else who wishes to join at 9.30; a private, privileged experience. The chapel is timeless, full of richly-carved oak bench ends, possibly from the Priory. The walls are whitewashed and the windows are clear except for one small coloured pane. The service is lead by Neville Chamberlain, former Bishop of Brechin, who is the present master, having taken over recently from Prebendary Parfitt, the fourth Parfitt in nearly 400 years. Sexey's Hospital is an embodiment of gracious, yet practical, community living.

At the eastern end of the town there is more visible decoration, some almost flamboyant. The pharmacy has a façade with plaster wedding cake swags above the windows and at the main crossing, a building dating from the fifteenth century — once four shops, now a restaurant — has an eighteenth-century pedimented porch, columns, pilasters and Venetian windows. Across in Abbey Fields, in 1894, King's School built, and still uses, a charming cricket pavilion; its highly-decorated white-painted eaves contrast sharply with the red-tiled roof.

But this is a mere sample of Bruton's seventy listed buildings, and along the Bartons — as in Frome, narrow lanes between houses — there is a much better view of the rear, often older, elevations. And as ever, one has to be on foot to gain an appreciation of the styles in the High, Patwell and Quaperlake Streets, where most of the domestic architecture has been re-fronted. There were silk mills in the 1700s employing upwards of three to four thousand people, some children as young as seven and eight. This forged a new wealth on which the population of the next century also thrived: Maton too confirmed that 'a manufacture of hosiery in Brewton and a great number of hands are employed in silk reeling'. But there is much more to discover in some of the timber-framed houses although many are medieval, there may well be older cellars — possibly Norman, perhaps even Saxon.

Bringing us back to the last century, like so many towns, we find that in 1931 Bruton was completely self-sufficient. For example Quaperlake Street had a bakery called Ovens, tearooms and a fishmonger, one of two in the town. Among the many High Street businesses and shops were a saddler, bicycle dealer, several grocers, a tea dealer, a plumber, watchmaker, the Bruton Brewery, Gas and Coke Co, and Co-op. Bruton Museum shows a good picture of its commercial and industrial past, at a time when everyone shopped locally because services and provisions were nearby.

Today many of us still want to do just this, but the car, one-stop shopping and the closure of some mills have taken their toll, although other additions help to cater for Bruton's 2,000 residents; (in the 1790s

Stone in its many guises at Bruton

according to Collinson there were as many as 1,500). A health shop is selling organically grown vegetables and a good range of groceries, however Windmill the ironmonger closed in the 1990s, has not been replaced.

When I met Mr Windmill in Bill the butcher's I asked him what, among his many memories, were those of John Steinbeck the Nobel Prize winner and his months at Discove, when he was researching Arthurian history for his version of the *Morte d'Arthur* in the 1950s. I asked him what Mrs Steinbeck bought, and he particularly recollected her first purchase of twenty-four coat-hangers, which I suspect indicated a wardrobe far beyond most villagers' imaginations.

As one might expect Bruton has a creative population, with a furniture maker, a sculptor and many painters. The Bruton Arts Society, founded in 1953, holds an annual exhibition at King's School each July. And Bruton also has an Arts Festival of music and drama during May, coinciding with the unique Packhorse Fair, with an exhibition to which many of these local artists contribute their Bruton-inspired work.

Steinbeck himself obviously loved this part of Somerset and immersed himself in the landscape as well as the legend: he wrote to his agent that he was 'looking out over the lands over which Arthur was Kynge'. He wanted to grow his own vegetables — he needed 'green' — and planned to grow climbing strawberries and train them up the front of the house. He felt that the 'pace of life' hadn't changed much, and with an acute ear he wrote that the speech was Anglo-Saxon 'with a lacing of Celtic'. As I imagine the lovely dialect peppered with 'thees', 'theys' and 'thiks' would have been more prevalent than it is now.

Mr Windmill still shops at Bill the butcher's, who seems to be one jump ahead of the local 'game'. Together with meat, they dry cure bacon and sell fish and vegetables, dairy products and just about anything produced locally. Bill 'flies the flag' and supplied local Dexter beef for HRH Prince Charles's visit to open the new Batcombe Village Hall a few years ago. He stocks the organic leaves that Charles Dowding grows commercially at Lower Farm, Shepton Montague where his wife Susie provides bed and breakfast of almost totally home-reared or grown content.

In this delightful valley they grow vegetables without spraying or artificial fertiliser. Guests are treated to their own pressed apple juice; Charles makes bread with wheat grown on his brother's farm and milled here; eggs are collected from their own chickens; soft fruit from their garden; Suzie makes her own granola and sometimes yoghurt; and the rooms are in a beautifully converted barn, light and private. I would like to wake up to the sight of their vegetable beds one May morning when the sun seems to make the asparagus grow in front of your eyes!

Castle Cary, Ansford and more villages

Visitors and residents alike walk along the Leland trail from Bruton, or take the train for one stop, finding the appeal of Castle Cary in its friendly scale; fine houses, mostly of deep golden Hadspen stone or Cary 'gingerbread rock' in a variety of styles spanning many periods. Its linear development does not compromise the intimate market place.

The words of the diarist James Woodforde are forever linked with Cary and Ansford, where he was curate. His diaries are a collection of the everyday; in particular they underline his interest in the food he and others consumed. Ansford, the adjacent parish, connects with Castle Cary on the northern axis; both in a landscape described by J.W. Collinson as 'situated in a very fruitful well-wooded landscape ... diversified with hill and valley'. If you live in either it is important to make the distinction between the two parishes, now only separated by two fields, one of which still hosts the autumn fun fair and the route of the October carnival.

Thus far Castle Cary keeps its market town atmosphere. It has not succumbed, as others have, to the lure of the large. It is principally Georgian, although many of the elegant fronts hide earlier houses. It was founded on the success of wool like many, but as wool declined so flax and linen succeeded. These industries, with twine, webbing and horsehair, are responsible for the wealth behind some of the wonderful architecture. From the top end of North Street, past Ochiltree House where the founder of the Macmillan charity once lived, the main thoroughfare changes name six times before finishing up at the top of South Street. South Cary also has houses that warrant a closer look.

We find that the town has evolved gently; a bright, sociable centre, much as it was, when the eponymous diarist was the curate. However, there is a good sprinkling of Victorian houses and the splendid flax mills — one was bought by Clarks in 1960, from the descendants of the Scottish entrepreneur William Boyd, who founded his company in 1837 off South Street.

As fashions changed, an elegant brick façade has been added to the stone of the Pines in North Street. The Methodist chapel of 1839 no longer has its Tuscan porch, but has a fine façade. Opposite, Ochiltree House, a long five-bay house with a pediment over the front door and 'generous' steps, surprisingly narrow for its length, was also faced with brick.

Just near the chapel, cleverly sited to avoid offending the illustrious neighbours, Cary's only modernist house has survived its first sixty years with an original wooden front door. The house was designed by William Albert Golding; drawings are dated 1946, London for Dr Lennie. The architect was born in South Africa, trained with Herbert Baker, fought in the First World War and designed this after he re-registered with the Royal Institute of British Architects (RIBA) in 1944. This small interloper has some Bauhaus design-attributes of wrap-around corner windows, and an externally rounded porch; otherwise the decoration is restrained, with only a small amount of surface brick pattern on the typically 1930s tower. The current owner has the original drawings, although the date for completion — at a time when building restrictions were still in force — is not certain. Although one could not call it a paragon of modernism, it is worth speculating how it came to be built when materials were in short supply. There is little wood. Perhaps the need for a Doctor's house outweighed these obstacles?

North Street, with its high pavements called batches, becomes High Street, and as we travel southwards there are several Victorian shop fronts, and a former Stuckey's bank, (now NatWest Bank), with the initials of the company ever entwined high on the front. Next the cobbled market square where the Market Hall of 1850 — a mix of French and Gothic by Penrose — replaced an earlier Court House. Here salsa and ballroom steps replace the dances and plays of the eighteenth century. South and central Somerset have a handful of what I call 'post houses', those that had earlier refined domestic lives; Wincanton has a dazzler — yellow-painted — in its market triangle. Here, behind Bailey Hill a high Georgian house of 1767 in Cary stone, with a tympanum above a central Venetian window, is the post office. Opposite is Cary's ancient scheduled monument, the most interesting town building. Called the Blind or Round House, it was put up in 1779 for £23 and is one of two in the county. Not so much a prison, more a place for cooling the heels of the drunk and disorderly. Appallingly, young children at the tender age of seven, who skipped Sunday School, might also be put here.

The path to the station in May

Towns that take you straight from the High Street to the surrounding fields always have a charm. By the side of the George, the last thatched building in Cary, with stone reclaimed from the castle, a narrow path called Paddock Drain leads up to Lodge

Hill. On special days beacons are lit here. Barely a mound now signifies the site of the castle. But at the top, among the grazing cows of Manor Farm, there are far-reaching views to Glastonbury Tor; to the woods at Hadspen; the ridged folds around Bruton; and the sight of at least thirty church spires to the north and west of the county. On a clear day there is also Bridgwater Bay and Devon further west.

Cary's, or Cari's, early history begins before Domesday; Michael McGarvie gives AD 725 as the date of the first Saxon charter. By 1086 it was a thriving agricultural community, with rich land and meadows abutting the 'infant' River Cary, whose source was, the now obscured, Park Pond. The castle may possibly be Norman, it became a stronghold of the Lovel family in the twelfth century, when the town acquired the Castle prefix. It was purchased by the Duke of Somerset after the reformation, (he also bought Glastonbury Abbey), then by Henry Hoare in 1720. Earlier we find that Charles II stayed here on his escape from Worcester having hidden at Trent. In June 1645 there was more action when there was a gathering by the so-called 'Clubmen' — part of the uprising by yeoman and farmers who had had enough conflict from both sides and wanted to safeguard their own land and property, sending a petition to Parliament to this effect.

James Woodforde was born at Ansford parsonage, a lovely house, still having its casement, leaded-light windows and an intriguing garden. He animates the years he spent between Norfolk and around Cary (between 1763 and 1776) in his diaries, in which meetings with the squire, clergy, publicans and merchants inform the social history behind these elegant buildings. He saw plays at the Court House, now the Market House, where among others *Hamlet*, *The Beggars Opera* and *Richard III* were performed to 'large audiences'. He attended dances at the Old Ansford Inn, now converted, and played the game of fives at Babcary in 1764 — his favourite pastime, also at Castle Cary's church and most probably at nearby Alford.

Cary was still dramatically active 150 years later. The 1922 yearbook of the Somerset Folk Society — of which, coincidentally, Douglas Macmillan was the general editor and director — recorded that the Cary Literary and Dramatic Society, formed to read the plays of Shakespeare, were still performing the pastoral plays, in the open air, up to the First World War. Their reputation was widespread. 'Am drams' are still popular, but more than likely these days the production is a twentieth-century musical rather than one by the bard!

Lower Ansford, formerly Lower Ansford Lane, was until the 1960s completely rural, with farms, orchards and barns where hay and apples were stored, mangolds were chopped, cider was made and horses were stabled. One resident, Stan Hicks, who was also born here remembers the smell of cider as it ran along the lane when the barn was cleaned out and the apples being unloaded! Beside the farmhouses were four weavers' cottages — maybe they wove sailcloth — and the first Victorian stationmaster and his assistant's villa. Happily there is still an orchard undergrazed with sheep, two fine early eighteenth-century houses with large gardens, and there are views over to Glastonbury Tor. At the end of the lane stone steps one hopes were trod by Woodforde, lead into Cary, now used by many who are walking or who arrive by train. Cary is unusually and fortunately near two railway lines with access to Bath and Bristol, Dorchester, Taunton and the West, and of course the metropolis if you need it.

Ansford parish church, St Andrew's — with a pinnacled-tower and buttresses — has views south and memorials to Woodforde's family, and this is where he also preached. In Cary Museum, tucked away up a stone staircase above the Market Hall, the Woodforde and Cary Preservation Society manage the collection of agricultural, industrial and geological artefacts, and the town's history. Farm implements cover one large area.

The story of Cary's industrial history includes the business of Thomas Donne who made twine and sailcloth from hemp and flax for 150 years. Their samples cards — craft pieces in miniature — would be sent out in advance or taken by the representatives to show the thickness, strength or patterns of the twine. The representative's calling cards were courtesy itself, written in copper plate. Customers were assured that 'any commands you may entrust to him [the rep] will receive prompt attention'. There are also samples and a history of John Boyd, who still make a fine material from horsehair and silk for exacting and prestigious clients.

People appreciate Castle Cary's independent shops. Yes, changing just as they change everywhere, but it is the service that pulls people in. Some have been in the same family for over 100 years, such as Lush's the butchers, since 1894 and Parker's the outfitters originating from the period. White's the former ironmonger served the town for over a century; the shop front is listed and the nineteenth-century tiles still add colour to the street, although the spiral staircase is no more.

Charlie Hill's pie shop

As Cary has always been self sufficient there are others: a large double-fronted grocer, a greengrocer, a fresh pie shop with a good window, antiques, several gift shops, a vintner, a delicatessen and another double-fronted shop, whose original windows with inset brass lettering provide the right milieu for bookselling. In 1831 Cary also had a bookseller, as well as twelve grocers. Moreover among Cary's creative population there are musicians, artists, writers and architects.

Past the Horse Pond in Church Street, the parish church of All Saints looks south to Lodge Hill and the cross, planted in hawthorn. Parishioners from all the churches walk from the Market Place on Good Friday in witness and gather for a short ceremony at the top of the hill above the cross. This church may have stood on the present site before the Norman castle and the first markets; what we can see now dates from the fifteenth century and is in the Perpendicular style. It has a clerestory and is embattled with gargoyles at roof level. The church was aggrandised by Benjamin Ferry in 1855, allowing at least another 300 'free seats' by lengthening the nave — generally giving the church a more 'slender and elegant appearance'. Being right on the edge of fields with trees planted for the millennium, it becomes another town stroll. Walking from here down South Cary Lane brings you to the flat lands and the hamlet of Cockhill, where a medieval barn, a bee house and a seventeenth-century stable have been converted for those seeking a Somerset sojourn.

Caryland is blessed with attractive villages, good churches, wonderful farmhouses and rich pasture. Although many of the dairy herds have been sold and the dispersal sales accelerate alarmingly, I can still sense Old Somerset as I travel through the villages over the moors to Glastonbury.

Just before Alford, I have stayed at Clanville Manor and now count as friends the Snook family who have farmed here for 100 years. The Georgian farmhouse of 1743, resplendent among the fields and farm buildings, is strategically placed for many of these excursions. The smell of hay that feeds their own beef herd, and the sound of chickens, which produce the breakfast eggs, the sight of the ducks on the pond as I first drove into the yard, coincided one spring evening with the arrival of the first house martins. Breakfast is wonderfully local: smoked salmon from Brown and Forrest, home-made marmalade, local cheese, bacon and sausages, served in a fine dining room with the fields which lead along a path to the site of an old Roman villa, seen through the elegant windows. Another, a round-headed Venetian window, faces the delightful polished oak staircase as you climb to the bedrooms.

All Saints at Alford, in Pevsner's view, 'is an uncommonly complete example of a perp church'. I admire its location off the road by the River Brue, near Alford House, surrounded by fields and ancient trees. This small church has a rood screen, a beautifully carved chancel roof and possibly later carved bench ends with poppy heads. Other natural motifs include a pelican, a dragon and a lamb with cross. It was restored by Sir T.G. Jackson, who also built the churches at Hornblottom and Lottisham for Godfrey Thring, the hymnodist and vicar of Alford, later made a prebendary of Wells.

From Hornblottom green and orchards, a pleasant stroll leads to the church of St Peter, designed in local stone by Jackson, a pupil of Norman Shaw. Built between 1872 and 1874, the interior is important, and surprising. The tile-hung belfry and the broach spire are both much more Surrey than Somerset and inside there is unexpected decoration of strawberry-coloured and white plaster ornamentation and figures on the walls. Jackson also designed the stained glass and chancel pavement. Further west, across the Fosse, the little church at Lottisham — a younger sibling of 1876 — has the same shingle-styled spire; in this case Jackson has absorbed and translated, in wood, the essence of a Tithe Barn. St Mary has a more rural, unadorned interior where the 'heavy rough timbers' of the tie beams and chancel arch express the vernacular forms of the farm-and barn-filled location.

Chapter 4

Somerton: former ancient capital of Somerset and Pitney

Glastonbury: peace, pilgrimage and the Chalice Well Gardens

Street: a good helping of culture, shoes and swimming

Lytes Cary Manor: a medieval house and gardens

Somerton: former ancient capital of Somerset and Pitney

*B*arely three miles beyond Castle Cary and Ansford, where memorably the older buildings are of golden Cary stone, the colours change. By the time I have reached Somerton, some ten miles away, all, or nearly all buildings are in silvery blue and grey from the stone quarried at Keinton Mandeville. Here one of Somerset's most famous sons, Henry Irving the actor, was born and spent the first three years of his life which a plaque celebrates.

Somerton's vernacular builders made the very most of their skills; there is a dignified air in parts of this former ancient capital of Somerset, a style, scale and architectural detail which elevate the town. Altogether the height of the houses, the width of Broad Street and the pollarded trees lend Somerton the character of a small French town. Happily, Ham stone dressings in the right places enliven the blue Lias on those Saturday mornings in the winter, when I am greeted by cold icy winds blowing off the Polden Hills.

Somerton is surrounded by pasture and woodland. South-east is the crossing over the River Cary. North is Littleton Hill and the Hood monument. All the features create an undulating panorama making the railway journey to Taunton a delight, as I can pick out all the church spires and monuments along the way .

Once past Keinton, a sight of Glastonbury Tor to the north-west, after a bend, and Kingweston, a rich and fertile arable area just as it was over 200 years ago when William Maton made his tour. He thought less of the buildings and much more of the grazing rights that the whole town of Somerton was able to enjoy on the west side. Somerton is on a slight eminence at a meeting point of several routes. My frequent approach from the east plunges me immediately into a surprisingly splendid urban layout without any suburb. With one or two exceptions, the original details have been respected by succeeding generations so that North Street, with low, two-storied terraced houses, offers the best introduction to the best detailing which proliferates in this town: delicate porches and a neat appearance. This leads to Broad Street with the finest houses, with more Ham stone dressings, see Craigmore House, the Natwest Bank (Stuckey's previously) and the Narrow House, narrow maybe, but cutting a dash with its round-headed Venetian windows. In this single thoroughfare where the market was once held, there is a bevy of bow windows, beautiful pediments, rusticated stone and quoins, elegant porches and old oak doors. Every autumn one studded oak door is brought to life with a profusion of Virginia creeper and hydrangeas, dripping pink on either side.

Elaborate drinking fountain

And there is more: wherever possible, the residents or original builders have embellished their houses or shops with wrought-iron work, so numerous balconies, fine railings and — at the junction of the tree-lined Broad Street with New and North Streets — an ornate early twentieth-century drinking fountain by Mr Head, ironmonger, commemorating the coronation of the new king in 1902 and heralding the Edwardian era. And it gives me pleasure to relate that opposite there is a good second-hand bookshop.

Somerton did and continues to welcome travellers, testified by the remaining numerous inns. But one important example is no longer an inn: at the southern end of Broad Street, adjoining the market place, stands what was once the Red Lion, described by Nikolaus Pevsner as 'the most ambitious of the Inns of the town'. The five-bay elevation has a large rounded archway, for coaches, and above is a Venetian window with broken pediment. Once the Inn had a large yard, now, inevitably, it has been developed into housing. How can we stop this downward spiral of developing every public-amenity building in every town and village? Barns were the first to become houses, followed by the creeping domestication of garages — small filling stations are a rarity, although there are more in west Somerset. And now it seems that every town-centre hotel, or old coaching inn, is vulnerable. Society still needs places to meet, socialise and debate informally, such as the pub or the market square.

However, all is not lost in Somerton: in West Street the Unicorn, developed in the eighteenth century, has probably the best and largest hearth that I have seen in the county. They burn two whole trees each winter day and host good music sessions! Even today, opposite the Butter or Market Cross, there are two of the original seventeenth-century inns, the Globe and White Hart. The latter has another welcoming fire, and was once the site of Somerton Castle, whose porch was still allegedly lying in a field at Chilton Polden in 1953, when Somerton compiled its useful coronation history.

It is almost impossible to conceive that the peaceful Market Cross, with its hexagonal roof and stone ledges for cooling butter, was occupied by John Churchill and his soldiers, over 321 years ago. In 1685 after marching from Shepton and Glastonbury, in pursuit of the rebels, and whilst trying to make contact with Lord Feversham, commander of the royal army, Churchill made his headquarters here on Thursday morning July 4th before what we now know as the Battle of Sedgemoor, which was mostly fought in the dark. Now, quite amazingly, also on a Thursday, the little building is filled with the blooms and colour provided by a flower seller. Such is the seductive power of history!

Somerton's built achievements are the successful knitting of ages, especially the space between the market place and the church. Opposite, in what was the old Victorian Court House, the Somerset Guild of Craftsmen, founded over 70 years ago, has just relocated its headquarters. With a backdrop of original features there are two floors showing furniture, ceramics, glass and jewellery, seen to their best advantage. This venue should become a catalyst attracting more makers to exhibit their exciting work, in a town location.

John Betjeman suggested that no English town is 'typical', and Somerton is far from typical of Somerset. For this small town, and the few that have not been decimated or suffered a character change through the onslaught of supermarkets, has a quiet, reassuring quality. Moreover the town's collection of doors satisfies one of my overriding passions — pure design history — a passion that is sometimes misconstrued. I am not casing the joint in a historic property, as a room steward wonders mindfully why I am fingering the door furniture — but I am admiring the hinges and escutcheons!

Doors do raise questions about the status of the owner of a house. Near the church there is an intriguing simple low door let into the wall on the east side; there are studded doors and double-studded doors at the market hall; and doors with classical porches, such as Craigmore House with its broken pediment on corbels. The Market House, north of the Butter Cross and once, I suspect, an Elizabethan merchant's house, has a superb six-panelled entrance door with its oriel and dormer windows above, reminding me more of the Cotswolds than Somerset, and this is the reason why it is the most individual house in the town.

It is only a few steps to the parish church of St Michael, an integral part of the scenery, occupying a beautiful setting, lying back from the market place, for Pevsner one 'of the most happily grouped urban pictures in Somerset'. In its own way St Michael has a 'close', not of ecclesiastical buildings, but rather of domestic houses. These contain it on the east and west, all behind railings, from which a long path leads to the south porch. Above this and on the tracery the Ham stone dressings shine in the sun and lighten the character of the embattled clerestory and tower.

St Michael is large and its carved roof is one of just three similar examples in the county. It has an octagonal tower, principally perpendicular, with an internal roof that is a *tour de force* of carving. Every inch is decorated: tie beams; king posts which meet with carved angels; and a profusion of tracery and decoration in the wall plates. Altogether there are 640 identical quatrefoil panels in the roof and yet another Somerset Jacobean carved pulpit.

Together with an early nineteenth-century Methodist church most of the town's shops are in old buildings: two butchers, and an excellent ironmonger-cum-gardening emporium; more a general store, even stocking real tin baking tins in every shape and size. Butchers sell local lamb and game, an arcade has among others, an independent health shop. And Emma B the award-winning delicatessen has recently branched out, opening a coffee shop within the Gifted Co's shop on the opposite side of West Street.

Of all the former WI or country markets this is the only one held on a Saturday in the county, hence early queues for excellent Somerset food; Jane Brooke and her family of Merricks Farm from Langport, sell only what they grow organically. You can find the unusual purslane, a sharp and succulent salad, whose praises both Gerard in the sixteenth century and John Evelyn in the seventeenth century sang: 'it is familiarly eaten with oyl and vinegar', wrote Evelyn, even then. There are baby beets, single serving cauliflowers, garlic and broad beans. Rocket runs almost throughout the year, red and green Swiss chard — a versatile vegetable — together with Somerset potatoes, blackcurrants and long stems of fennel all in summer. Slender bunches of celery — so full of flavour and crunch — confirm the season and winter solstice, when real celery is pulled and of course squash — where would we be without these many-hued and shaped stalwarts of the post-Christmas kitchen? Two or three excellent plantspeople come here and the baking, especially the shortbread, is buttery and the marmalade, tart and chunky. Phil and Jo Hillard from Pitney sell their welded toasting forks, solid steel garden and plant supports and, excellent sweet pea plants among many others.

A few miles west there is another hostelry that is made for a cold night; it has several log fires, the mummers come singing at wassailing time. There is a large choice of dishes: of sausages and mash and others of gargantuan Somerset portions. Running north just before the Halfway House a lane leads to the pretty village of Pitney and a sign for the Pitney Farm Shop. Lizzie and Rob Walrond subscribe to the ethos I have been spreading through my work with my clients for years — trying to cut food miles — the villagers who walk here get a discount! Pitney's farmyard is a pleasure: the hens run in their field and the blue and natural timber shop is at one with the beautiful rolling landscape near Langport. This indigenous little shop has been constructed using as much farm-found materials as they could possibly lay their hands on.

The family have been farming for generations. Along with their eggs, pork, lamb and their popular sausages — Pitney porkers — there is some amazing green back bacon, their own vegetables, (respecting the season); the precious leaves of new salad, when plentiful, are laid with care in local baskets. Among the other local produce, they sell both the apple juice and ice-cream made in this same village, named after Manor Farm's Jersey cows, Ermie and Gertie.

From Pitney, with its church and nearby Roman villa, my

road often leads me to the hills, moors and rhines of Low and High Ham. Make no mistake, this is a prime example of 'finds' found when diverting from the main road, although this is B category; even better leave the car before you enter for a charming perambulation. Only in this way will you discover more of the village, grouped as the Saxons always formed their settlements, with church, cottage and manor still unaltered 1,000 years on.

Glastonbury: peace, pilgrimage and the Chalice Well Gardens

'There are many reasons', wrote S.P.B. Mais in 1934, 'why you and I should go to Glastonbury — the Musical Festival [that of Rutland Boughton], the attraction of a smiling countryside, architecture and archaeology; but there is also this reason — here is the Holy Grail, here lies King Arthur'.

It took almost ten years before I made my own appointment with the Abbey ruins one late December morning. The moment had to be right for what I knew would be a powerful experience. I also waited to make my first steep climb up the Tor, with a friend one bright February morning when, true to Somerset form, a hailstorm chased around our heels as we struggled to the top. Another awaits me — over the whale-like hump of Wearyall Hill, which in John Powys's *A Glastonbury Romance* is climbed by moonlight. Traditionally, this is where Joseph of Arimathea plunged his staff into the hill, where it took root and continued to flower once at Christmas and again in May.

Glastonbury is packed with legend, myth, ruins and festivals but it is a living, breathing town. There is an open-air market and the country market in the Town Hall on Tuesday, and the Farmers' Market was one of the first in the county. Some of the faces in the High Street and market seem to have stepped out of the pages of Powys's extraordinary novel; the traders could well be descendants of families who have been bringing their goods and produce from the villages on the moors for hundreds of years. And so Glastonbury fosters friendships with a tangible acceptance of whoever you are or whatever you have done. It must be the common purpose of pilgrimage in all its guises that has created this easiness.

For my Abbey visit I chose a winter day, three after Christmas.

Market Day

The ceremony of cutting the holy thorn had been and gone. It was sub-zero but the view through the railings in Magdalene Street was mellow in the winter light; and the copper beech leaves near the Abbot's kitchen still shone. These ruins are surrounded by four streets: at the south-eastern corner the Abbey Barn, at the opposite north-west corner the Market Cross, a slender neo-Perpendicular Eleanor cross by the architect Benjamin Ferry, of 1840. In its earlier form it resembled the wool market at Dunster. South-west there is a park, and at the north-east, the main approach to the High Street with a bite taken out of it, there is Silver Street. In this corner within the wall, the nineteenth-century Abbey House was built with much of the original stone, as was much of the town. Nevertheless the sense of a separated relationship between the Abbey and town, although they would have been interdependent, is still strong.

The Abbey was built in 1184, replacing an earlier one destroyed by fire in 1120. This was once the greatest monastery in England and has the reputation of being the site of the first Christian church in England. Like many others it was razed during Henry VIII's dissolution.

The progression from the gatehouse is through a modern building with an exhibition interpreting the site's history, with a south-facing window that introduces and frames the north wall of the Lady Chapel and the surprisingly beautiful gardens. As you walk on, you realise that yours are only two among the millions of feet to have travelled thousands of miles over thousands of years. Just before the door to the Lady Chapel a large cross with a sign reads, 'Christian sanctuary so ancient only legend can record its origin' and no more is needed.

The language of the Norman carving is arresting, as is the craftsmanship and geometry. Carving of this quality on the west front at Wells is too high to appreciate with the naked eye but here, above the lower wedges of this doorway worn by weather, the higher sections of the thirteenth-century voussoir are easy to read. We see carvings in relief that include the Annunciation, the Visitation, one of Herod's soldiers on horseback and it is supposed that St Bridget is the woman milking a cow. Within these ruins I found more round-headed windows than I had expected — cleverly described as 'Saxonico-gothic' by William Maton — but there are also pointed arches and plenty of the zigzag decoration that is so typically Norman.

Your feet take you on through the former nave, and under the extraordinary fractured ruins of the crossing tower, and one tries to imagine this being much higher than the tower at Wells. One continues to what was the quire and chancel, altered by Abbot Bere, who inserted the scissor arches at Wells. It is interesting that the very processes of deterioration allow us to see the construction of the massive wall; the cutaway dressed blocks of stone reveal the rubble core behind. Looking down from the seat at the end of the Edgar Chapel, there are glimpses of the old town chimneys and nothing else spoils the view, aptly described by Mais as this 'palimpsest of red brick on haunts of immemorial antiquity set on the side of a green hill'.

As well as the famous holy thorn, *Crataegus monogyna biflora,* there are stately trees which have matured over hundreds of years — holm oaks, ilex and blue cedar are just some of the 261 species listed in these thirty-six verdant acres — and orchards. The latter were replanted as recently as 1975. The monks would certainly have made cider. West of what was once the monks' kitchen, a herb garden has been planted, with feverfew, wormwood, rue, mint and betony, all playing an important part in the daily round of living and caring. Two seats are also modern replacements: one woven in willow, with a double-pointed back capturing those older stone shapes, the other, with a decorative back, has been woven like a cobweb.

Now for the *pièce de resistance,* the Abbot's kitchen, the most important intact building of its kind in the whole of Europe. With an oven in each corner this would have been both a hive of activity and a hothouse; truly a medieval catering kitchen, used solely for the needs of the Abbot and his guests.

Firstly look up at the ribs of this building. These taper from the square base measuring sixteen feet, at ground level. Smoke passed upwards through a double octagonal vent which crowned the summit of a pyramidal roof with the same number of sides. To give us a better view, the custodians have thoughtfully fixed a mirror to the base of an old walnut tree, secured with the wheel of the first motorcar owned in Somerset, by Squire Greville of Butleigh. Formerly there would have been a granary, for large amounts of bread would have been baked; there would have been a larder for the game from the Abbot's seven parks, which were full of deer; perhaps a brewery and a cellar for the wine they produced. Spices would have been ground in the large mortar on show, recovered from Butleigh. Whilst fish caught in the Brue were kept at the Meare Fish House across the moor, which still stands today. There was, according to the Commissioners writing to Thomas Cromwell at the time of the dissolution 'a great mere well replenished with greate pyke, breme, perche and roche'.

This is the largest and possibly the only ecclesiastical kitchen of this design, a design entirely appropriate to the Abbot's status. From here the individual courses for feasts and dinners, including game with fish and bread, were taken only a few steps to his hall, where he entertained. He was permitted to do so because St Benedict's strict rule had been altered to accommodate this lifestyle, far richer, of course, than the food prepared in the monks' kitchen for their refectory.

How this remained undamaged, whilst stone was taken, and perhaps sold from elsewhere on the site, is astonishing. Certainly this extraordinary building, with decorative gargoyles and buttresses, carved windows in the upper lantern and corbels outside the main door, is a building of its time fit for purpose. After the destruction of the Abbey, the land and the kitchen changed hands many times over the next 450 years — once being used as a Quaker Meeting House — until the whole Abbey was given back to the church at the beginning of the twentieth century.

Tudor Rose on the Tribunal

Between the fifteenth century and the 1950s, when John Steinbeck came here, researching his *Morte d'Arthur,* many writers and topographers have left their impressions in ink. Mais, once headmaster of Sherborne wrote: 'Glastonbury is a place of pious pilgrimage' where, the legend says, Joseph of Arimathea landed (it was surrounded by water until the monks started the drainage) with his eleven companions, carrying 'the Holy Chalice out of which our Lord drank at the last supper'.

In Maton's eyes Glastonbury was 'equally interesting with any in the West'; we should add England and even the world. He also noticed that most of the town's buildings were decorated with the spoils of antiquity, and what had been the Abbey gate had become an inn and a hospital. Over the last two hundred years we also know that Steinbeck, Mais and H.V. Morton were among the literary travellers who stayed at what Maton described as the 'curiously ornamented' George. The many niches and carvings on the façade of this former Pilgrim's inn are more sumptuous than its purpose signifies. He, like me, did not see the thorn in 'fructification', and supposed that it had been introduced from the east.

Of the many celebrators of England who have inspired me, Morton in 1927 summed it up: 'it is perhaps not strange that all places which have meant much to man are filled with an uncanny atmosphere as if something were happening secretly; as if filled with a hidden life'. He ended, 'I have been to Glaston'. So have I. The uplifting power of that 'hidden life' remains with you for some time afterwards.

Pilgrims have also been drawn to the Chalice Well for millennia; for the curative powers of the water, the timeless feeder spring and the legends and spirit, with which Glastonbury is inextricably linked. Small wonder therefore that people become 'companions' of the captivating Chalice Well Gardens with its magical and peaceful qualities.

The well and the surrounding gardens are managed by a Trust formed in 1959. They call this 'a place whose history has no beginning'. But archaeological explorations in 1960 suggest that the well chambers were built at the end of the twelfth century with stone, possibly reclaimed from the first Abbey. A dig in

1961 exposed a large taproot of a yew tree with its water content confirming that it was growing here in AD 300, when the country was under Roman occupation.

Wherever the healing water flows, from the chalybeate spring source, through to the drinking pool and flowform, installed in 1933, its route is coloured by red oxide. Trees enhance this liquid energy, as do perfume-giving shrubs, herbaceous plants and landscaping. Meandering paths, tranquil arbours — often circular — and curving borders are incorporated. And at the entrance and arrival there are concentric motifs, sometimes with a central ammonite — as many have been found on this site — which are devices that recall the hillside context and the well's interlocking symbol — the Vesica Piscis. With the first spring sun almost every blade of grass, leaf, and bloom shines, as if polished. The yellow dwarf tulips, 'Giuseppe Verdi', a startling red *Chaenomeles japonica* and clumps of soft yellow primroses, glisten. And nearby a Holy Thorn, one of three in leaf, bears the visible buds of its first, twice-a-year flowering, underplanted with winter aconites.

In the herbaceous borders white and blue pulmonaria bloom and within the shade of the magnificent yews, hellebores and acid-green euphorbia flourish. Behind a seat in the corner border of the drinking area called the Lion's Head, the first delicate leaves and buds of *Dicentra alba* thrive on this well-mulched soil and you might see the leaves of papaver, iris, and the more advanced aquilegia. You might also catch the delicate, china-blue flowers of the *Corydalis flexuosa* 'Père Davide'. But for intoxicating spring perfume, the numerous plants of daphne have, for me, no equal.

The gardens are linked with Chalice Hill, passing through a hazel tunnel and a growing apple arch, which opens onto expanding wildflower meadows, with a viewing seat commemorating the millennium. To sit here or by one of the wells is to relish time, looking and drinking in the vistas towards the horizon-breaking Tor, or west to the expansive panorama of the Somerset moors.

Street: a good helping of culture, the shoe museum and swimming

Glastonbury and Street are very close. They share the same moorland views, both had sheep-derived industries, they even shared venues for Rutland Boughton's famous 1920s music festival and from this Street has developed its theatrical activities. Each has their own different character and this is what attracts me to both.

However people only see Street as a fairly modern town and may not have read as much about it in conventional history as about its illustrious neighbour, but it is not without history. A Roman road ran from here to Ilchester that may have connected up with the road leading to the lead mines at Charterhouse. And if we travel further back, hereabouts one of the oldest fossils of a striking giant lizard — the *Plesiosaurus* — was found in the Lower Lias. Lias is particularly noted for its ammonites and other fossils.

The mud and clay from the earlier wearing away of limestone was deposited in the shallow sea occupying this flat, middle part of the county, even the top of Glastonbury Tor is also partly formed of this rock. Street's built character is wholly formed of this grey local stone, which the town's exceptionally bold, street blooms enliven in the summer. The stone was so abundant that you can find large slabs, often seen in old cottages, also used as upturned fencing, by talking a pleasant walk up to Overleigh.

Street was recorded in the Domesday survey. There is Ivythorn Manor, built by Abbot Selwood of Glastonbury and a thirteenth-century parish church that once also belonged to the Abbey. Friends who live here love the location, and I can see why; you can cycle straight out from the town, or walk, along droves and across moors. From Walton Hill there is a marvellous panorama of Dundon Hill and High Ham. Wildlife abounds: one week seemed to have made a whole season's difference when I saw, on my usual route through Baltonsborough, that the cows had been turned out, the willows were greening and the swallows and spring had arrived!

Whilst it was solely concerned with farming and quarrying, the greatest social changes occurred in the mid-nineteenth century, when Street became a 'company town'. Company, however, hides much more than it may imply.

In 1825 a family of farmers and graziers undertook an early nineteenth-century equivalent of diversification. Cyrus Clark finished his partnership with Arthur Clothier to become a fellmonger, skin and wool dealer and rug maker. He took in his brother and made his first steps into footwear in 1833, and they made lined slippers, using the smaller rug skins. So an empire began.

It is important to remember that the business of C. & J. Clark is embedded in the Quaker ethos, so concern for every aspect of the welfare of their workforce — from education to leisure, from health to happiness and housing — was paramount. These ethics directly affected the town's growth — the majority of residents worked for C. & J. Clark — the pattern of its public buildings and the image of Street, and of course to a great degree the workers' attitude to their compassionate employers. The architectural effect of this underlying paternalism was as sharp for me when I first saw Street, as when I saw New Earswick at York, created by Joseph Rowntree with the same spirit of philanthropy. The houses in Wilfrid Road, almost opposite the factory, are perfect examples of pleasant, company housing with good front and back gardens for growing vegetables.

Back at the east end of the 'village' the Clark's-funded Victorian buildings can easily be picked out. Firstly there is a mid-Victorian Friends' Meeting House, built in 1850 by Frank Cotterill, which pays its respects to Georgian elegance. Next, built in the year of Queen Victoria's Diamond Jubilee, the centrepiece of the High

Street: the principal factory building with a tower designed by George Skipper, supposedly a copy of the castle tower at Thun in Switzerland.

This empire is best chronicled at the nearby Shoe Museum, really one of the best in the country, which explains the story of these beginnings and the development, with some astonishing variations in design, of the humble shoe. The Museum is located in part of the original factory, opposite the Bear Inn, once a 'dry' pub, or rather the Clark's 'temperance-coffee-house' answer to alcohol, not taken or encouraged by Quakers. The Bear, once a simple thatched inn, was much changed in 1894 by William Reynolds, who remade the façade adding some charming windows and late Victorian comfort.

Skipper, whose famous work in Norwich is the flamboyantly baroque Royal Arcade, also designed the Crispin Hall. This community club and lecture hall, opened by John Bright the famous liberal, now needs some restoration. He also built Millfield, a large house for the Clark family and the building from which Street's large, public school took its name.

1920s Queen Anne revival window

I was intrigued to find that Clark's patronage of art, architecture and education covers a whole gamut of styles and talent right up to the present day. For example the piece hanging in the main reception, opposite the Museum, by the African artist El Anatsui is a compelling, bright work that covers a large wall. Resembling an eastern cape, it is in fact made of thousands of bottle tops linked together. Earlier, in the mid-twentieth century, such artists as Richard Naish, David Tindle and Kenneth Rowntree were commissioned to paint views of the factories and surrounding landscapes, perhaps in some cases idealising the subjects in that 'between-the-wars' and 'post-war' evocative genre. From an earlier decade the library has two pencil and pastel portraits of William Stephens Clark and Helen Priestman Bright Clark made in 1912 by the portrait artist William Strang, whose work also hangs in the National Portrait Gallery. On the same wall, above the Laurence Housman collection of this prolific writer's work: plays, illustrations and fiction, there is a portrait of him by Cecile Crombeke. Housman built a house for himself and his sister in 1924 called Longmeadow, where the garden building he used for writing, the Elbow Room, still stands. And the view of the fields and trees seen through the wooden pillars on the veranda would inspire him today. I enjoy using this library, built in 1924 with original window seats and the hexagonal table, once belonging to William Stephens Clark of Millfield.

Millfield School are themselves major art patrons and in 1992 they opened the Atkinson Gallery, with a mandate to promote young artists and bring an international calibre to the south-west. Regular exhibitions for the public, some very cutting edge, include works chosen from the degree shows of MA students from across the country. Moreover their sculpture park is a beacon for the region. A work on loan by the eminent Anthony Caro, and Peter Randall Page's Millfield Cone, can be seen with twenty-four other works around the 100-acre campus; many by winners of their international open competition.

So Street's cultural life is growing, with an art gallery, a sculpture park and a modern theatre complex — Strode Theatre — adjoining what was once the technical, now Strode College. This shows a programme of both English and dynamic foreign language films, more diverse than the surrounding towns, and attracting wide audiences. It also has a reputation for musical theatre and pantomime, performed by the students and other companies, with a large local involvement just as there was at the

1920s music festivals. In the spacious theatre bar area local artists are exhibited in rolling exhibitions and there is always the chance of some lively debate with other film buffs afterwards. You can also drink Hecks apple juice. Hecks is the second oldest family business in Street, making cider up at the farm in Middle Leigh for well over 100 years.

But we have waited long enough for the Museum, which so admirably charts the C. & J. Clark history and also shows arguably the largest collection of shoes in the country: both their own designs and gifts and items from around the world. I believe this

18th-Century ladies shoes and shoe buckles

makes a good design and social and economic history resource.

I suspect 'The Fitting Story' which opens the exhibition on the ground floor, will bring back memories. Shoe-fitting equipment held a fascination for me, especially that X-ray machine, which has since been banned, and the sliding foot measure, for width and length. In the former one saw one's feet and bones, lit up at the base of the machine and looking quite other. Ponder this. The child was the centre of attention and, usually, a lady devotedly brought out any number of shoes from hidden depths: seeking out the right size, the suitable colour, the suitable style (about which parent and child did not always agree). The opening of boxes, the rustle of tissue paper, shoe horns and the smell of new leather … I found this small theatre captivating and evidently aspired to being a 'shoe lady' myself for a short time. Stylish shoes still have a place, among my country, walking boots.

From a well-designed entrance, and oak staircase, we arrive at the cases of shoes from foreign lands: an Indian lady's wedding shoe, highly embroidered; Egyptian bootees; a North American boot made from buffalo hide. Not foreign enough? Well here is a Russian slipper, *très moderne* — post revolution — and there, recovered from many centuries past, a Roman girl's shoe — from AD 350 — excavated from a site at Low Ham in south Somerset and unbelievably a classic bar-style, in the truest sense and still made today.

A red velvet shoe with a high heel dating from 1660, of the Restoration period, begs the question: was height important socially, or politically in the seventeenth century? In fact I discovered that the high heel served a more practical purpose, helping those who were walking or marching to keep their boots mud and water free. This dovetails nicely with the first skirmish of the Civil War fought earlier at Marshall's Elm, just south of Street on the way to Somerton, when 600 foot of the Parliamentary infantry, marching to capture a body of Royalist horse, were ambushed by Cavaliers and seven men were killed.

By 1690 men's and women's shoes had become extremely pointed, with buckles or ties. From this period and for the next 150 years every piece is hand stitched in tiny stitches even on heels; stitching of the kind seen on linen rather than leather. In the heavily-laced era of the mid-eighteenth century, shoes became more dramatic: a white mule of 1760 has a floral design beautifully stencilled. Some have sequins, sprays and spangles, with the skills of the embroiderer as evident here as in clothes of this period.

A pump dating from 1815, with ties, reflects the dancing and society that is rife in Jane Austen's novels and the Victorian age of travel, is represented with more sensible high button boots needed by both sexes. Among the thousands, and for the new spectator sports of the 1930s, I managed to find a lido shoe made by Bata.

And now for a swim. Cross the road to Greenbank Pool, the outdoor pool or lido opened by Hilda Clark in 1937, who was carrying out the wishes of her sister Alice. She wanted the young ladies of the village to have better opportunities than swimming in the River Brue offered. This is actually where the young lads swam and the local paper — reporting the opening ceremony — mentioned the hints made about naked bathing at Clyce Hole! Every year this wonderful pool opens in late spring — an eagerly awaited event.

But interestingly, Greenbank, beloved by all who swim here,

Greenbank Pool

including this writer, is a work of modernist design; one of the rare extant lidos left in the country. It is the only example of its type and period in Somerset — where once most towns had one, most are now built over! (Shepton Mallet and Portishead still have outdoor pools, but neither have this setting.) And if confirmation were needed that a well-thought-out design lasts, this does so. Jack Stock designed the changing area and filter room and Mr A.J. Taylor of Bath, the pool itself.

Parents and children love the pool, where many generations of the same family have learnt to swim. Little has changed, except a shop added in the 1960s and some water-play equipment. It is now listed, with the original classical lettering, seen in the opening newspaper report. The open-air changing rooms have been modernised, but we can still dry off in the sun. Where else can one see grazing cows while one swims? Moreover as grass and trees surround its thirty metres, the original intention to provide health-giving sunbathing is as popular as ever. Some of us are proud to know the elderly gentleman in his 90s who travels from Bath, to swim and soak up the sun.

The Hecks family certainly have proof that late spring has arrived. When the pool has opened I become a summer migrant, calling in to their farm shop, hair wet, after a swim, to the barn up at Middle Leigh. Here I buy their Tor apple juice, (sometimes a blend of Cox and Bramley), some Green's Cheddar, and if the bees allow, a jar or two of honey.

Lytes Cary Manor: a medieval house and gardens

To the Dovecote

Lytes Cary Manor is situated south of the Cary to Somerton road in a sunny landscape with the River Cary lending its name to the house. The Lyte family first built their chapel in 1348. However Lyte, meaning little, was first recorded in 1255 and is a name found only in the south west.

Thomas Lyte built his Manor House in 1460, which the family beautified and enlarged for the next 200 years. But they left in 1755 after the house had begun to fall into disrepair. Until 1907, this little jewel languished, becoming in the most part a farm store, not unlike Barrington Court. In this case it was purchased, rescued and polished by Sir Walter

Jenner. Though ruinous, it has not been ruined by any heavy-handed restoration.

The medieval Lytes had royal connections and Henry Lyte's translation of the *Niewe Herbal* from the Flemish in 1578 and his son Thomas's book, are important works of history. But without Jenner's restoration of the house, in the Arts and Crafts tradition, assisted by his architect C.E. Ponting, we could not so easily conjoin history with fabric. Lytes Cary is one of those manor houses — like Vann in Surrey, restored at the same time by W.D. Caröe — where the scale is pleasing and the original areas and the restoration blend perfectly. In 1949 Sir Walter bequeathed his much-loved house to the National Trust.

From the farm buildings, passing the early twentieth-century farmhouse, the house is entered through a stone porch with an upper oriel window. Sir Walter inserted the screens passage – one would have originally separated the kitchen from the great hall. The hall's beautiful roof comprises three tiers of curved wind braces with angels supporting a shield showing the Lyte arms at the base of the rafters. Sir Walter collected furniture of the right period, the seventeenth century, which is well-lit by high windows with stained glass. And a copy of Henry's famous Herbal, lent to the Trust, is on show, under glass.

The adjoining Oriel Room shows the development of early dining rooms in the mid-sixteenth century, as yeomen were breaking away from communal eating, which had taken place in the large hall. In Jenner's time there were, and are now, elegant views of the Apostles — twelve clipped yews — lawns and the dovecote obscuring the well. Lytes Cary has no mains water as yet.

Although Sir Walter found the sixteenth-century great parlour being used as a farm store, the original panels, Ionic pilasters and pillars had been painted over. His restoration has given us a real sense of the life of Somerset gentry in the sixteenth and seventeenth centuries. There are vistas from the large windows and Sir Walter's carefully chosen objects, textiles and furniture, are mutually complementary. The beautiful seventeenth-century stump work is an example: embroidery worked in relief, over blocks of wood or in some cases padding, to give a three-dimensional effect. Here it surrounds a seventeenth-century frame, added to by Mrs Leopold Jenner, Sir Walter's sister.

With this exceptional piece she made her contribution to the room's historic and aesthetic qualities; combining a view of Lytes Cary with her own house, Avebury, also restored around the same time. This was a talented and artistic family. Sir Walter himself played the piano and made recordings. He also composed an opera about the Duke of Monmouth, possibly based on the play written by Laurence Housman — then living in Street — that was performed in Bristol in the 1930s.

In 1967 the house was the subject of an essay by Christopher Hussey in *Country Life*. The magazine's founder Edward Hudson, whom Jenner knew, had a strong influence on other Edwardians in the crusade to preserve England's domestic architecture by illustrating similar country houses in the early 1900s, championing the Arts and Crafts movement.

The little parlour takes us back to Henry Lyte and his son Thomas. Here they may have studied, writing their antiquarian publications. Then the tour ascends to the great chamber where the remarkable plasterwork ceiling executed in 1533, is of a style not usually seen before 1580, making it one of the earliest examples of a coved and ribbed ceiling in Somerset. In this ceiling Sir John Lyte showed his loyalty to the throne, by incorporating the coat of arms of Henry VIII.

And the garden: how did it look in Henry Lyte's day (around 1578) when he translated Dodoens' herbal? John Aubrey, distantly related to the Lytes, noted that around 1660 'Henry had a pretty good collection of plants for that age; some few whereof are still alive'. As it was probably a Renaissance garden in structure, it may not have looked dissimilar to its present form — with the herb garden and farmland close by as they are today. Sir Walter designed the garden but may have been influenced by Thomas Mawson, a contemporary designer with a theatrical style. Jenner's garden had many of the features Mawson used in his popular Arts and Crafts style: a series of garden rooms, bordered with yew, and walled areas to increase the drama.

With the exception of the vase, main and herb gardens the bones are original. The main border is a *tour de force* of thirty-five metres, and was first created by Graham Stuart Thomas 1964. Biddy Chittenden and her husband conserved the colour plan when they replanted this in 1996. She told me how, as tenants over forty years, they also created the meadow-like orchard with dramatic weeping ash tents, replacing elm, reminding the viewer of the countryside's proximity.

The south-facing border scheme of over eighty numbered plants has colour and form to satisfy every taste. We are taken through blue echinops, hibiscus and cerinthe to pale lemon argyrantheum. After cream and apricot we reach the pinks, reds and mauves via lathyrus, roses, penstemon and phlox. Under the arch the eye comes to rest with a calm coda in the white garden, replanted by Mrs Chittenden in 1999.

With the support of the Trust the Chittendens imaginatively removed hedges so that there is one continuous stage set from the fountain garden to the house. They also made the geometric planting of the lavender and herb gardens — linking with Henry Lyte's work. These beds make rich feeding for butterflies and bees and one good summer — the humming bird hawkmoth year — we saw them *en masse* on the lavender. This fascinating species can migrate from Spain and France, with ensuing generations maturing here and, as the name suggests, they hover like humming birds, feeding with a long proboscis.

In this same area, in late summer, tubs are planted up with the highly-scented, beautiful *Gladiolus calianthus*, white petals with dark red markings. And for more perfume, walking past the tumbling *Trachelospermum jasminoides* in a small hidden corner is a heady experience. I have been trying to encourage one on my front arch, but as Simon Larkins the head gardener has told me, it needs shelter to perform like the specimen at Lytes Cary.

The Trust has compiled a small leaflet describing a mile-and-a-half walk around the estate that reinforces the local ecology. Another restoration project, but here one for the benefit of wildlife and riverbank habitat as well as visitors. Ambling through the meadow planted alternately with medlars, quince and apple trees, walking the *allées,* or looking north from the fountain, shows us how Lytes Cary's gardeners and designers have managed the change from formal to informal with consummate skill.

If Lytes Cary has inspired you to buy some examples of what they grow, they sell their own plants and hold special plant sales days. But do also travel just a few miles south to Kingsdon to see Patricia Marrow's nursery. 'Patty's Plum', the stunning papaver, was named after this distinguished Somerset plantswoman whose knowledge, unusual stock and advice has, for me and other plant lovers, been of great value.

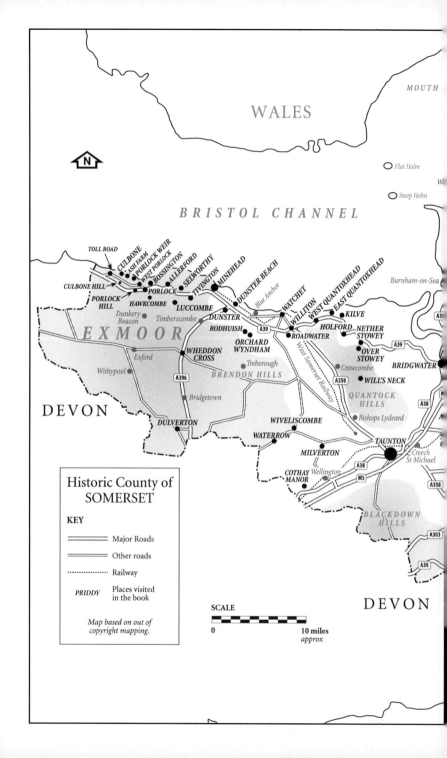

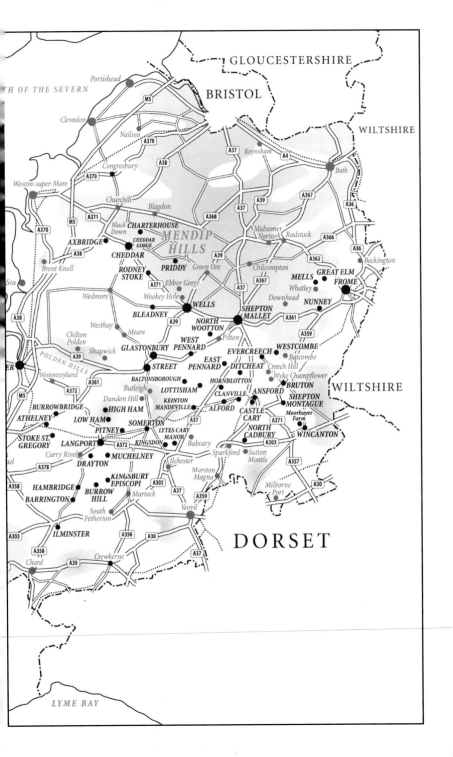

Chapter 5

Much to do in Muchelney: the Abbey, the Priest's House, the Church and the Potter

Drayton, Hambridge and Kingsbury Episcopi - a delicious food loop

From Barrington to Ilminster

Langport, willow and Burrowbridge

Much to do in Muchelney:
the Abbey, the Priest's House, the church and the Potter

*I*n her *Somerset* of 1949, I believe Sylvia Townsend Warner found the heart of the Muchelney matter when she wrote: 'One has never seen Sedgemoor until the greater part of it is under water, once under you can appreciate its delicate economy of feet and inches above sea level'.

Unbelievably there is too much history at Muchelney, a very small village, which in 1795 had thirty houses. The land around Muchelney is breathtakingly beautiful in spring encircled by orchards of apple blossom — Walter Raymond's 'blewth' blossom — in turn grazed by fattening sheep. But somehow winter brings me closer to the past, when the bleak mist, rising from folded pasture can change instantly with the light and liveliness of the floodwater. Then the familiar round tops of pollarded willows rise up from a bright blue surface on a sunny December morning, transforming the gloom of a previous muddy afternoon.

This region makes one aware of the forces of nature. When the moor is under water, the smallest hill becomes a safe harbour for cattle. A lane just a few inches above pasture becomes a causeway for two, or four-wheeled travellers between 'lakes' to the next village. And Wet Moor Lane reminds me that gambling on a short cut is not worth the odds. The doors of the ancient Priest's House and older Abbey are closed to visitors, but the leafless isolation resonates better with the medieval period; a time when the monks of the Benedictine order peopled and cultivated the lonely 'island' in Sedgemoor. Certainly the hospitality they gave those who braved this triangular piece of land encircled by the rivers Yeo, Isle and Parrett would have been gratefully received.

The 'ey' of Muchelney is Anglo-Saxon, meaning the great island. Muchelney does indeed become an island when it is cut off by rising water: winter vegetables become waterlogged and it was not unknown for kitchens to be flooded, or for villagers to have to row across fields to get winter supplies, or in the extreme, to be rescued. The great flood of 1929 remains in living memory but now the management of these surrounding wetlands, lying only inches above the sea level, has outwitted nature, to a degree.

I found the local saying 'Coat goes first and Muchelney follows' an actualité, one Saturday in December when I was bound, first, for Kingsbury Episcopi, and its market. When I doubled back and arrived at Muchelney, the fields in front of the Almonry Barn Café — once part of the Abbey, but converted to barns in the sixteenth century — were under water, the pollarded willows just showing their crowns. I was snug and safe, with a pot of fresh coffee, and a wood burner, the waterside panorama, the sun shining on Langport to the north and the tower of All Saints, I felt this was all mine.

Across a field to the Abbey and church

The reason for the early monastic settlement, a fraction higher than the rest of the village, in what we might call inauspicious land, is open to speculation. Did the prospect of lush summer pasture outweigh the isolation and water of the winter? Whatever the reason, we have to admire their forethought and the legacy of a rich concentration of historic buildings, giving us the remains of the Abbey, the parish church, Priest's House and Almonry.

Chronologically, we should begin at the Abbey: the oldest building in a village where there are the remains of the once-great monastery, Abbot's hall, church barn and the reredorter. Not as large as Glastonbury, which was the first of all the great abbeys, but the Abbot of Muchelney also needed a wide-ranging organisation to carry out the reclaiming of land to increase the pasture and provide his income. If you have a passion for worn stone steps as I do then explore the Abbot's House. In terms of wear they probably equal those extraordinary steps which lead you up to the Chapter House at Wells Cathedral; uneven wear as one would expect, and in this case more wear on the left ascending up to the parlour, passing a quatrefoil-headed window.

In this hall the Abbot would have eaten, entertained, greeted and welcomed his guests; perhaps they were seated at the long settle that is built along one wall and two corners. A roaring hospitable fire would have burned in this splendid fireplace, winning Pevsner's praise as 'one of the most sumptuous pre-Reformation fireplaces in the country'. The fireplace has an intricately-carved stone relief above the piers, with large lions couchant, looking outwards from two; the noble hearth is flanked either side with John Leach's timeless pots and vessels. And the heat from large logs would have dispelled the inconvenience and damp vapours of a journey over water and windy moor.

It is generally thought that King Æthelstan first founded Muchelney Abbey in 939. At one time there may have been as many as 800 people worshipping and working in this inhospitable place. However there was a settlement here as early as the sixth century. The so-called Black Cannon monks raised pigs as well as sheep. They grew strawberries and grapes and this cultivation is evocatively represented in a painting on the ceiling of the east room. They ate eel, improved the land, grew herbs and distilled remedies, thus keeping themselves fit as well as ministering to their guests. Perhaps they caught and ate wildfowl or mutton from the marshy swamps, packed with wild thyme flowers which were sometimes made into a pudding. And they drank cider, wine and mead in many forms, from light, made with pure honey, to strong: 'fine metheglins flavoured with herbs and spices'.

The skeleton of the medieval range shows you what materials were used. And the Abbot's house helps to illuminate the skills that went into the construction: in the east room there are elemental cross-banded wooden beams, and a wagon roof. We are shown the priorities — shelter and warmth — for from below the heat would have risen, warming and enticing the visitors with the cooking from the early sixteenth-century brick-backed-hearth in the kitchen. This is a space whose original design is not yet totally resolved: there are remaining lintels placed in odd positions in the walls above the 'hatches' which cannot be explained. But elm plank doors and a chimney hearth, wide enough to step inside carefully and peer upwards, are more than enough.

As for the carvings, these are a pictorial history of the everyday: for example a sixteenth-century loaf and a flagon of ale, which was a gift from the Abbot to the parish priest who lived in his self-contained house across the field. Whether founded by King Ine or Æthelstan — antiquarians cannot agree, it was, like so many others, dissolved in 1547. On the other hand unlike others, the secular buildings are intact because the Earl of Hereford took over the range and re-erected a Manor House; it was a working farm when William Maton made his tour around 1795, shaded by 'venerable old elms'. Much of the stone that went missing has been returned. The cloister can still be seen, but nothing of the Abbey Church stands above ground, although for the archaeologist the exposed foundations offer much to pace around and consider.

Back past the reredorter, the two-storey building which houses the latrines and wash house, the road leads to the parish church of St Peter and St Paul, once separated only by feet from the old Abbey transept and the southern end of the Abbey Church. The painted Laudian angels in jewel colours, with fine gold stars, against a blue, white-puff-clouded sky in the nave, are cheeky and naively worked — their voluptuousness makes a soft contrast with the precision of the fan vaulting in the tower.

Opposite there is a house. This is one of the most beautiful, small medieval buildings in the county — the Priest's House built in golden Ham stone for the incumbent of the church around 1300. Once a hall house it is by no means small, more akin to a yeoman's residence. The front elevation positively sings with two double-height windows and tracery that compares with examples in the Abbot's House. The following may explain my fondness. It is not just the age, stone, purpose and history but also the twentieth-century additions, made in perfect synergy by the architect Edward Barnsley. He had set up workshops in the Cotswolds at Daneway House, Sapperton where he both made and showed his furniture. Barnsley's additions became what The Society for the Protection of Ancient Buildings (SPAB), who bought the house in 1901, advocated — seamless, as seamless as William Morris and Thomas Hardy, who both helped with the purchase, could have wished.

Barnsley made the repairs to the buildings, safeguarding its future, and gave it some twentieth-century comforts. His new works are a kitchen dresser in elm with a long centre drawer — heavy to use no doubt, and three corner cupboards. Look at the pattern of the nails, the hinges and catches and the play on space in one corner cupboard; designed apparently on the slant to make optimum use of an awkward area. These handcrafted, functional designs complemented the elm, Tudor ceiling and are the embodiment of the Arts and Crafts designers' philosophy.

In this house all the early twentieth-century additions have a use. Without pastiche, it venerates old crafts, where each element expresses function, skill and construction. For some ten years an architect and his wife, who once lived at Daneway House, lovingly looked after the Priest's House and showed scores of visitors around, including my daughter and me. Outside the house there is an enclosed garden, with a seat on which to sit and look at the church and orchards, whilst waiting for one's turn to visit the small house.

One October on the last showing day we walked from here, passing the Abbey towards the Pottery located among the scattered farmhouses — beautiful in their own right, often thatched and mostly built of blue Lias with Ham stone dressings and hood moulds. The Pottery can be found on the road to Kingsbury.

This is the home and studio of John Leach, who started working in Muchelney in 1965. He is the eldest grandson of the world-renowned potter Bernard Leach, who founded his Pottery in St Ives in the 1920s. With his team, John makes the firing day for the new kiln, in autumn and spring, something of an event. John has also made a wildlife sanctuary with 4,000 broadleaf trees and a pond, thereby repaying nature that has provided him with wood for the kiln for the last thirty years. The shop, full of his wares and some willow pieces by David Drew, is always open and there is a gallery where other artists show their work. On firing days, visitors are tempted to buy a pot or two and taste some of Julian Temperley's exquisite Pomona aperitif, served with a morceau of Brown and Forrest's smoked eel or cheese. Leach's shelves and tables are laden with brown, earth-coloured pots: soup bowls, plates and salad bowls, used by some famous restaurants for decades — such as Cranks — and gracing many a farmhouse table.

These vessels await fillings of golden butter or clotted cream, a cream which would flatter the strawberries grown by Helen and Graham at nearby School Farm House — continuing the centuries-old tradition, as seen in the monk's mural. At a lovely old thatched farm, with a brick front, on the bend just before the Pottery, they also grow vegetables and perennials and sell from a farm shop. You will recognise the smallholding by the huge stacks, or arisings, of wood in the yard!

Muchelney may seem like an escape, but this is the reality of Somerset with its absorbing, unexplained past. Who really knows what happened in the Abbot's House? Whose idea were the cheeky angels? If such mysteries are the essence of Somerset, so too are the craftspeople and farmers who work with the land which is ever fertile, ever enriching the taste, be it of cider brandy or strawberries. Whatever the weather, the kiln has to be fired to bake the pots, which should be filled with soup — soup made from local produce.

Drayton, Hambridge and Kingsbury Episcopi – a delicious food loop

Ordnance Survey maps are absolutely indispensable. They give us remarkable topographical clues to the locale we want to explore. But they cannot tell us everything about the food we might encounter on the way. The map for this journey marks out many farms but only one has a signifying tag line — for the cider mill at Burrow Hill. Below there is much more.

This delicious food 'loop' starts a mile beyond Langport, to which we return later, and should include Merrick's Farm, for Soil Association-certified, vegetables, found at Somerton's Country Market. Staying on this farm in a converted stable, perhaps hiring bikes would be a superb base for the following. Soon a sign directs you to Drayton — a set back, but well-set-up village with a perpendicular church and a stumpy tower, venerable houses and cottages, and a summer fair along the whole length of Church Street and School Lane.

Drayton has been immortalised by the artist Dick Sturgeon, who was born here in 1920 and later lived at Curry Rivel. Sturgeon knew what to celebrate — the vernacular he lived among which pleased him most. But I have also discovered that the village had its own resident photographer, Harry Stone, who between the late 1880s and 1930s recorded all the scenes of everyday life that made this working village.

Back to today and the work is only to travel and taste. Drayton's was the first village produce market to open in the south Somerset area, inspiring Burrowbridge and Barrington to follow suit and, most recently, Kingsbury Episcopi. The market is held in the old schoolroom, to which producers and makers have been coming for the last eight years, in the company of Stone's images, which hang on the walls. Pauline Fisher, who lives here, told me that the interest generated by the food stalls at the late, August street fair in 1997, spawned the ideas of a village market. So Pauline invited villagers to bake on a regular basis and continues to attract other

producers.

The doors open on the third Saturday of the month at 10am and some brisk trade takes place. Pauline makes delicious pork and chicken pies, with a light pastry and a hint of juniper. It is best to order or arrive early for these! She also slices and sells wedges of Cheddar from a whole truckle, made by Keen's of Wincanton and the much younger Westcombe dairy — another award winning Cheddar — and also Somerset-made Caerphilly from Duckett's; (we met them all in Chapter Three). Bakers from the village include Santa Checkley who creates delicious savoury morsels and, among others, creamy chocolate confections. The sum is good — as good as I would expect to find in a first-class delicatessen or in the market of a small French town.

There are the familiar faces of the Small family from Charlton Orchards of Creech St Michael, who travel to many Somerset markets. During winter they bring some of their thirty-two varieties of apples, and juices. In summer they bring soft fruit trays of three coloured currants and herbs, before the first English apples arrive.

Dodie Huxter, who once farmed at Muchelney, now in Crediton, brings lamb as well as rare breeds' meat such as Shetland — a very lean and close texture, full of flavour — as well as beef from their slowly matured, Red Ruby herd. And Helen or Graham Walker have a table of their vegetables, summer fruit and beef from their Muchelney smallholding, depending on the season. Graham can be easily spotted with his milkman's leather bag. Mary Powell's lemon curd and apricot and almond tarts are very popular, whilst Brigit Aita, also from Muchelney, shows her hand-painted silk scarves, and cards. I could buy just about everything I needed for the weekend but suggest arriving with an open mind. Not knowing what you are going to find is one of the true delights of going to market! The bonus here is good coffee and maybe a chance to talk to a retired farmer.

Wandering through this tranquil village, the church, thatched cottages and thatched war memorial remind us that after the Second World War, in which he was taken prisoner, Dick Sturgeon came back to Somerset — which he always wanted to be near — to train as a fine artist. There were no spaces on the courses of his choice, so he trained as a commercial artist at Bournemouth College and later at Taunton. He worked for the *Somerset Gazette* and took up sign writing, pub signs and the sort of gilt lettering that solicitors have on their windows. So private commissions followed and his late start developed into a prolific career, in a particular genre: watercolours of cottages and cottagers that had been in vogue twenty years earlier.

Just a handful of food miles, by way of Midelney — the back-way for cyclists — the road leads south to Hambridge. A few yards on the left and a slight incline, brings one to Bowden's Farm where Brown and Forrest run their successful smokery. The unprepossessing converted barns and outbuildings give no outward sign of all the goodies within. Since the 1980s Michael Brown has been smoking eel and other fish; last year's harvest from the River Test was the best ever. Once young elvers were caught from the Parrett during spring, in great quantities and made into a cake. And we know that the monks of Muchelney were harvesting 6,000 eels a year from their two fisheries. I had my first taste of smoked eel as a child when I was encouraged to try a small amount that my father used to buy from a continental delicatessen; I imagine it must have been quite a luxury, but like all good tastes you only need a sliver.

As well as eels, Brown and Forrest smoke chicken, lamb, salmon, haddock and trout, cheese and quite amazing fat bulbs of garlic, which are hung over the oak and beech chippings. But a shining, simply-furnished restaurant is the other wing of their family business. Red check table cloths, fresh flowers and often a small exhibition on the walls make a good intermission for eating and relaxing whilst taking this local food excursion. This is as informal as eating at home with good friends, but here the smiling staff do the work! Utta Brown has devised a short menu which wisely concentrates on the food that they smoke here, served with a good salad, potatoes and rye bread. But the puddings can be comforting: baked, bread and butter, served with golden syrup or 'boozy fruit jellies'. Both my friends and I find that the homemade brownies melt far too easily.

Across the way in another barn, Richard Dennis, a collector and publisher has opened up a marvellous shop selling British-made studio pottery. The names roll for the pottery patriotic — Stabler at Poole, Hugh Casson for Midwinter, Eric Ravilious for Wedgwood; just some of the examples that reign resplendently among odd pieces of pressed and fun glassware. In terms of groaning tables of ceramics, this is an Aladdin's cave, and a bright one. The shop has large windows — the sun floods in and frames the next landmark of Burrow Hill with one tree atop, in the parish of Kingsbury Episcopi.

Burrow Hill is a proper topographical beacon, highlighting

some of the best taste in Somerset and has become a much-loved landmark. It rises up 200 feet out of the orchards and moors directing me to Passvale Farm where Julian Temperley's famous cider apple brandy is made. This is the only licensed still in the south west, and one of only two in the country which visitors can see working, through a plate glass window. One called Josephine was made in 1932; the other answers to Fi Fi and is slightly younger, made in 1948!

One summer Saturday afternoon I found myself accidentally travelling, behind two sides of Morris men, whom I passed as they stopped to dance in front of the Hambridge Inn. It was outside the rectory in 1903 that another well-known folk occurrence took place. Cecil Sharp, collector of traditional folk songs, was visiting the rector and heard the gardener singing 'The Seeds of Love' in the garden. His name was John English and from this seminal moment a new form of social anthropology was born.

I arrived at the farm ahead and started to taste, then the two Morris sides arrived, *en route* to a convention in Bridgwater. Whereupon Julian and his family invited the dancers to join a family birthday party being held in the garden. And so it grew. I watched and soaked up this serendipitous moment – cider and Morris dancing could not make better partners.

At the back end of another year, around the middle of December when the harvest is almost completed, the farmyard is full of apples. They are piled up in crates awaiting the press. Now is the time to taste, and buy maybe; some of their three, five and ten-year-old cider brandy or an aperitif called Kingston Black, (a blend of Kingston Black cider brandy and apple juice) — perhaps drunk on a summer evening and served ice cold — or the classically named Pomona, the colour of dusky topaz. But you can always taste at any time of the year in what were originally old threshing barns; all is wood, all is fairly dark, but far from dismal. Gloom cannot coexist with the smell, taste and colour of the cider and cider brandy, the bottles and the barrels.

And then a family with younger children came in to enjoy the multi-sensory experience of the barn, and the aromas, which will, one hopes, stay with them for years. I must add that their lusty lip-smacking approach to apple juice tasting was no less serious than the adult imbibers!

Julian passed me further on the loop to Carolyn Perrin whose daughter Sam was working for him. The following week I travelled to meet Carolyn, one of the farmers who rear cattle on these pastures and sells beef — Herefords crossed with Black Angus, (possibly of Viking stock), and Charolais — at the recently opened market at Kingsbury Episcopi. This is held on the first Saturday of the month in a red brick, gothic Victorian schoolroom, having the bonus of the luxuriously decorated tower of St Martin as its neighbour — all in a street where you can still hear cattle.

Carolyn brings beef from Lower Burrow Farm; such cuts as rump-skirt need slow cooking with a bed of onions and carrots, even cider. On a December day there were vegetables, including red onions, carrots and parsnips from Muchelney, pork from Orchard Corner, local cakes and preserves. To finish, why not chocolate made by a chocolatier who brings her beautifully presented bars from Sutton Montis, near Cadbury Castle. This company, like the market, is in its infancy and I hope they both succeed. The signs of another burgeoning food and social mixing place were apparent, as old recipes and cooking methods inspired by the produce were topics of conversation. As a bonus, for the folk-life collectors, Kingsbury has its own street fair on Mayday with traditional maypole dancing.

The more I meet these farmers across the whole county, the more I sense the unwritten code of co-operation that oils the sometimes difficult wheels; one will turn up in a tractor to help another, as if by some magic. As Carolyn told me, this close-knit community of farmers 'are only kept apart by water'.

I have realised why choosing food this way gives me so much pleasure, no more than the food deserves, but it is the thrill of buying from the growers and makers that I love most. The talk animates the transaction. It is alive, with a minimum of wrapping, the antithesis of what some call the chore of the weekly shop. To use a musical analogy, I could not work without the inspiring music of BBC Radio 3, but a recording, however accomplished, cannot be compared with the involvement of live music making, or a performance such as one given by the students of Wells Cathedral School.

From Barrington to Ilminster

There is a perfect, straight cycle or drive from Hambridge, past the white wooden mill and alongside the former canal to Barrington. This is an attractive village with stone cottages, thatch and a thirteenth-century octagonal church spire. The village farms, except for one market garden, have gone and so has the model farm built in the 1920s at Barrington Court at the other end of the village. But the Elizabethan mansion, in Ham Hill stone set in 220 acres, and an example of beautiful high Tudor style, is open.

Barrington Court, built by Henry Daubeny, the first Earl of Bridgwater, in an almost symmetrical E-plan shape, heralded the forthcoming Renaissance. The splendid porch is three-storeyed above the door, rising up to the dormer level; with finialled gables, so much admired at the time when this and the Priest's House were saved. It was in an appalling condition, without the balustrades or any of the features now seen. For this we owe a debt of gratitude to the Society for the Protection of Ancient Buildings (SPAB), who raised public awareness of the sorry state of some of our finest heritage.

Barrington was acquired by the National Trust in 1907, their first country house and yet another that would have disappeared had it not been for a wealthy benefactor. Here it was Miss J.L. Woodward, who put up £10,000 towards the cost. However more was needed and its future was not secured until after the First World War, when in return for a long lease, Colonel Lyle, another benefactor, saved, restored and added much to the house and gardens.

There are orchards, extensive parkland and formal gardens which owe much to the designs of Gertrude Jekyll. And the walled vegetable gardens are a horticultural work of art; more so in the late autumn when the bones of the espaliered, apple, plum and pear are revealed. In the house, late Autumn opening offers more room to see the timber panelling, linenfold in the Hall and in the staircase; both came from other houses but are stylistically and historically correct. Now it is let to a company of craftsmen furniture-makers, who recreate Jacobean interiors for historic houses and churches, and who have imaginatively made a display of Jacobean elements of churches and houses in Somerset. This gives visitors a pictorial pointer to the whole period.

In 1919, at the time of the rescue of the Court, the village was not doing well. Robert Dunning tells us that 'the greatest barrier or enemy of education was the blackberry'. That autumn the chair of the board of guardians and the schoolmistress gave up the unequal struggle of getting children to attend school. A bumper crop was a real contribution to the family food supply and income as the children picked 356lbs of blackberries in three weeks!

Today, although Barrington is another shopless village, a group of enterprising residents have set up a village produce market which goes a little way to restoring this loss. Like Burrowbridge this venture was underpinned by fundraising — needed in this case to build a completely new hall that is planned to open in 2006. It only takes one vase of sweet peas on a seersucker-covered table to encourage customers to sit down and discuss the market delights and the smell of fresh coffee which organiser, Leslie Jones, readily serves. The Legge family, who have one member living in the village, bake their bread at Martock and have done so since 1914. Without any additives, they bake cottage loaves, cobs, granary and split bloomers – even corn bread; this table alone must be a great boon.

Next by way of Stocklynch or Whitelackington and Dillington House — where music, lectures, conferences, and art are promoted — to Ilminster, the town serving this southern boundary of the moors. Its special character is derived from the local Moolham stone that shimmers in varying shades from gold to dusky topaz depending on time of day and weather. After a shower it glints. The residents of larger towns could be forgiven for looking enviously at what Ilminster has and how this stone was used. At the centre is a fine minster church, a small close of medieval houses and opposite a wonderful survival of a nineteenth-century department store. On the cultural front there is an early, eighteenth-century Unitarian chapel, now an arts centre, and Ilminster has a theatre as well as an idiosyncratic little auction house.

When the writer M. Lovett Turner moved to Ilminster, just before the Second World War, she realised as I have done, that if you want to see Somerset beneath the skin, the farms and farmhouses, it takes time. She had, as editor of a county magazine, the land and farming at her heart; with this in mind she commented on the pace and will of a herd of cattle that had better ideas than the herdsman in the 1940s. Why not thank the farmers who remind us that we are in the country!

Ilminster, I am told, has changed little over the last seventy years. Now of course there is piped water (rather than the well that supplied Lovett Turner's family), pumped by the same septuagenarian who, with his elder brother, also pumped the organ at the church. They may have stood side by side but had not spoken for seven years! Lovett's family walked from the single-track station whilst their luggage was taken in the horse-drawn station bus. The horse's days were numbered, soon to be replaced by a dark blue van, and the station is no more.

But today, travellers in the know take one of the Berry's coaches that run twice daily, through south Somerset from Taunton to Wincanton. Cleverly, this family-run company carries you to London without hassle. It is one of county's best-kept secrets and engenders the kind of bonding that stagecoach travellers might once have experienced. No scrambling for seats: civilised conversation and attentive service bring like-minded people together. I number two Berry-made friends from this neck of the woods, from Barrington and West Lambrook. If you look up at the side of the George, much reduced in size now, you will see a sign that tells of an eighteenth-century horse-drawn coach that departed from here, twice daily, even then. It was here that the infant Queen Victoria experienced her first night at a hotel, with her parents, on the way to Sidmouth in 1819.

The 'Minster of the Ile' – with its twelve pinnacles, the town's history, the arts centre and Ilminster's civilised service need some enjoyable time. You will find this kind of service most noticeably,

at R.A. Dyer, an exceptional draper's store opposite the church. It is so much appreciated that when it closed for ten months in 2005, the populace almost grieved. Barely forty years ago every town in the country had such a store of outfitters and house furnishers. They are part of our heritage and those that remain, like ironmongers, surely need saving.

Many of the houses have fine door lights and porches and many shops retain their original windows, but the façade of Dyer's in Silver Street also keeps its original sweeping, Art Nouveau, green-painted fascia, with brass door furniture and pleasing exterior mosaic floor. Inside all is wood: the floor, the glass-topped showcases, the half-circular cash desk and the bentwood chairs, placed at each counter for the comfort of the customer. The gentlemen's department is going strong; farmers travel from west Somerset and further afield for their country cords and shirts. And having recently been redecorated, the ladies floor is now open again. Along two sides of the first-floor showroom I counted thirty-four large wooden hat drawers, each one numbered consecutively in gold.

Ilminster prospered in the eighteenth century — when 1,000 pieces of narrow cloth were produced — followed by collar-making in the 1870s, an industry which employed three to four hundred women. This economic buoyancy contrasted with the effects of the agricultural depression in nearby villages.

Today the butcher and greengrocer support local producers, selling cheese and crops from the area. Ilminster has a bookshop where you can browse and an independent pharmacy that also sells tickets for the Warehouse Theatre — promoting the town's arts, whilst dispensing potions. Before long it becomes apparent that everyone in Ilminster has the town's best interests at heart.

Ilminster was once a property of Muchelney Abbey, and the first parish boundary was recorded in AD 725. The first market is noted in Domesday and even earlier, a charter was granted by King Ine in AD 785 for a sheep fair, always held in the last week of August. The open Market Hall, of around 1813, that we now see in East Street, would have replaced a shambles some 100-feet long that once filled the street. However, the size and quality of the Minster's decoration, from the late medieval period, is the overt history of the town's prosperity. Apart from the church, most buildings date from the great conflagration of 1491 when much of medieval Ilminster was lost.

There then followed some of Ilminster's most important, historic moments when the Duke of Monmouth sought support here for his bid for the crown. He attended a service at St Mary's and then passed through again on his way to the Battle of Sedgemoor. Ilminster and its townsfolk, like other parts of the county, suffered much from the ensuing reprisals.

However, there could not be a more tranquil space than the interior of this beautiful perpendicular church. Built in the hey-day of English parish church building, 1450, the two-storeyed tower and long-transomed window lights echo, on a smaller scale, the tower at Wells Cathedral. Inside one sees exceptional fifteenth-century memorials to Sir William Wadham and his wife and the seventeenth-century memorials dedicated to his descendants, Nicholas and Dorothy Wadham. In his *Churches of Somerset* Kenneth Whickham praised the latter: 'there is no finer post-Reformation brass in England than that of the founder of Wadham College'.

Much later St Mary's was endowed with a distinguished millennium commission: a pair of engraved glass doors were funded by a local family and made by artist Tracey Shepherd. This engraving is a beautiful marriage of message and motif that has been cut onto a pair of double doors, sharing divided messages. On entering, one is met by the greeting prayer: the annunciation enclosed by the sun motif. On leaving, the left hand door offers the blessing of peace, read from the nave interior with the accompanying moon motif. At this point there is a simple sprig of symbolic willow which, with a larger branch, reminds everyone who enters the church of Somerset.

Before the common possession of clocks, a particular ring of church bells might give secular messages, such as gleaning and harvest time. Here the so-called pancake or shrivening bell was rung on Shrove Tuesday to bring the congregation to confession, before the first day of Lent. It was rung until 1891 when the custom lapsed, and rung, I was told, just once again in 1996.

Walk around the close, the tower, transept and Wadham Chapel, the chantry, and Crosse House to see these and appreciate them as a very attractive group: the latter with its later double-columned porch was once the boarding house for the Grammar School, founded in 1549. Further along the north side, one finds the converted school and then Church Walk leads pleasantly, back to the Market Square.

Time to see the art and take coffee. At the top of the hill at the Meeting House, the former chapel provides long tables for café conversation; they make their own scones and soup and the coffee is good. An eclectic range of events is mounted in the main body of the church, including antique fairs and music workshops. Ilminster fosters the work of the large number of local artists through this centre as does Dillington House, both venues for Somerset Art Weeks. But of course you can plot your own trail every two years in September to hundreds of studios in the county.

Langport, willow and Burrowbridge

Langport is another jumping off point for the journey across the moors and south. It is a pleasure to spend time here, using the architecture to interpret the past. This tells us that Langport was once a market town, a very important port and a centre for Sedgemoor. And as a Saxon *burh*, built on a causeway, it had its own mint. From the outlying villages of Curry Rivel and Muchelney, villagers would walk to shop and trade at the market. There is just one main street, Bow Street, where a resident, born here, informed me that as a boy in the 1930s he remembered that along this length one could buy anything and everything.

Langport has always looked outward across the moors and beyond to the sea for its trade, surrounded by the rich common moors where commoners can still graze their animals. The relaxed air of the town comes from its position on the River Parrett; you can almost feel the sea as you walk along the riverbanks and meadows. The great Parrett not only provides a rich habitat for wildlife from source to mouth, but was also the means of voyaging out. It hardly seems possible that at the beginning of the last century travellers could buy one single ticket from the combined solicitor and bank office to take them to Bridgwater, then Bristol and so on to America!

As much as 500,000 tons of goods were brought to the port, transferred to barges and thence taken across Somerset, even before a new bridge was built in 1844 — a bridge engineered by William Gravatt, who had worked under Isambard Kingdom Brunel. The tonnage was made up of stone, bricks, coal, culm, flax, flour, sugar and one of the mills held salt. Then shipping started to decline with the arrival of the railway — Langport had two stations and the main route west still runs through the town – but alas, like so many other Somerset towns, the link has been lost.

However, the elegant houses and shops in Cheapside mirror the pre-railway buoyancy, in particular those of two families — the Stuckeys and the Bagehots — who were making their name in the early 1700s. These two families were responsible for the early eighteenth-century coastal and river navigation trade and through marriage they formed the formidable banking dynasty of J. Stuckey and Sons in 1826.

Thomas Bagehot worked at the first branch and his famous son Walter was born there, but the Palladian-style bank building we see now, formerly Stuckeys was built as late as 1875. It is faced in ashlar stone with a well-studded door. As a company Stuckeys were 'lavish' in their choice of styles, decoration and materials.We see evidence of this in many Somerset towns. As the bank was the farming community's most favoured and trusted, it thus became the largest in the county.

With the closing of the river trade and the wharfs, Langport's star fell, but it is beginning to shine again as more buildings are restored. In Bow Yard near the former salt warehouse, a creative new development of light, airy and sustainable, eco-friendly houses has been built, facing west, making the very best of the water and moor aspect and swallowing the sunlight. And the same organisation is restoring the salt store as workshops and studios.

If Langport's latest additions get our support then the town should be on the way to recovering its shopping prime, both for food and culture. Firstly, a new fish shop has opened — the reverse is usually the norm — and secondly a bookseller is putting Somerset at the top of the list. And Sue's Pantry, an enterprising food shop, moved from

The River Parrett, a lifeline for wildlife

its small beginnings into what was once the Langport Provisions Stores, where all the gold lettering and mahogany shelves are put to their rightful uses. Not only do they sell many organic groceries but also every kind of nut, seed, dried herb and fruit. You can buy any quantity, which is weighed out from the long line of jars and handed to you across a matching mahogany, former bank counter. With these and other traders, Langport locals have a choice: two butchers, a working silversmith, an enamalist, fresh flowers in the Guildhall undercroft, antiques, bakers, a small country market and other open-air stalls on Fridays.

Take a stroll along Bow Street and you will see any number of fine houses, some in brick, some with pantile roofs, some painted, some with mansard roofs, others can be glimpsed through courtyards and iron railings. Many are in the essential blue and grey Lias, picked out with Ham stone dressings and porches. Then look down also at some of the unconverted courts or yards to glean some of the industrial past. Opposite the bank the arcaded Georgian Guildhall or Town Hall occupies the focal position. This housed the court, two lockups and the cells and has a lantern and weather vane dating from 1733. At street level the three arches, faced with Ham stone, lead to the town garden and moor.

Further east, the post office, once the doctor's house with a fluted-column porch and perfect entablature, also took Pevsner's eye, along with the Langport Arms. Here, the abundant crops of willow grown on the moors were once auctioned.

And then a goodly climb up The Hill for an even greater range of styles; one Edwardian house makes a visible change with its tile hanging, peering over the steep street and not far from the church, in what could be converted stables, another shows how the builder has gone to town with the decorative brickwork.

Whoever chose the location for All Saints chose well. This is the best hill-top spot with the Hanging Chapel and medieval gateway a little further on. This is the best place to see out over the flooded moors in January. The church is managed by the Churches Conservation Trust and consequently only opens on request. But I recommend collecting the large key from the Retreat opposite, to see more. The church is mainly of fifteenth-century construction, with a remaining Norman lintel above the carved south door — stunning and decorated with the most unusual surface carving, incorporating very large leaves around the head. The church is spacious with north and south aisles and with tall windows in the embattled chancel. One finds some of the best examples of original stained glass in the county in the east window and the whole has boxed pews.

Walter Bagehot, one of Langport's and England's nineteenth-century luminaries, was buried here in 1876. There is a double memorial to Bagehot and his wife which was restored a few years ago by *The Economist*, where he once worked. His reputation survives, not just as a political economist and moral philosopher, but also as editor and director of this political publication. He was educated here in Langport Grammar School and became a brilliant scholar. Gordon Lee, himself a former senior editor of *The Economist*, in his monograph *Voice of Sanity*, explains the respect that Bagehot won here in Somerset and throughout the world. He writes of the young Woodrow Wilson, who, before becoming President of the United States and architect of the Versailles Treaty of 1919, visited Bagehot's grave in 1896. He cycled from Wells to pay his respects to the man he called 'master'. Bagehot eludes categorisation: a hard rider, lover of nature, brilliant journalist, biographer, a banker of course, and one who could add voice to the contemporary progressive thinking of Darwin, but with his own inimitable quest for the balance between 'progress and stability'.

I am not so sure if we can claim progress in the case of the number of hectares of willow crop that used to be grown hereabouts and inextricably bound with Langport. But possibly the largest concentration of willow still growing in Somerset can be seen along the Stathe to Burrowbridge road. Follow more causeway-like lanes alongside the river where the fields are punctuated with corrugated sheds or ivy-covered brick chimneys — the old withy boiling houses, which are now industrial archaeology.

As for stability, willow needs balanced wetlands, here drained by a hierarchy of small ditches, larger rhines and the large drains, so this region is perfect. Harvesting takes place through winter; withy cutting has to be finished before the trees bud again. On wind-blasted days the industry is busiest — cutting, measuring, bundling and working noisily — for the hurdles that are made in the sheds at the English Hurdle Company at Stoke St Gregory. Here you can see bundles or bolts stacked in all their green, buff and brown glory.

Willow was a perfect building medium. Think wattle and daub. And medieval architects and builders could use it for scaffolding, as well as carrying stone and sand. Moreover few tools were needed for its harvesting — the same applies today for the tools and for the finished objects. Every imaginable vessel is still made for catching, carrying, collecting, storing and caring. The sixteenth-century basket-makers' coat of arms was a willow cradle. Withies are malleable and many-hued and complement food. Surely, a white and buff willow basket, nursing a cache of speckled brown eggs, is right.

Author's own woven laundry basket

Only sixty years ago the carts that delivered peat to many of these cottages delivered it in bucket-shaped baskets, made by the basketmakers that lived and worked in the area. Some of the twentieth-century objects, such as flying machine seats used in the First World War, together with the growing and making processes, are exhibited in the small museum at the Willows and Wetlands Visitor Centre at Stoke St Gregory, where the Coates family have had their business since 1819. The patterns are timeless and willow has its own vocabulary. Both the names of the species, Black Maul, Champion or Viminalis, and the making words such as 'randing', 'upsetting' and 'waling', sound ancient and Norse-like. I did literally try my hand(s) at making a linen basket over two days at the Rural Life Museum in Glastonbury. It was tough, I had to think with my fingers.

Willow has been woven through our literature from Chaucer's *Miller's Tale* to W.S. Gilbert's *Mikado* and *Patience*, from Shakespeare's *Hamlet*, to the poet Thomas Chatterton, a Somerset son. In 1620 that great recorder of English husbandry, Gervase Markham praised 'Osiar [which] serveth for making baskets, chayres, hampers and other countrey stuffe'. So 400 years later we love and use our baskets, for shopping, laundry and yes, hampers!

Many artists are inspired by willow and the other Somerset rural industries of apple growing, cider making and the ancient tradition of catching elvers on the River Parrett, which just survives. I first saw Kate Lynch's work in the restaurant at Brown and Forrest near Hambridge. It was her image of an elver fisherman with his light shining, miner-like, down onto the catch — magically capturing the Somerset sky at night and the night worker below — that grabbed my attention. Kate and her husband James live at High Ham and both, in their own distinctive styles, celebrate and show us the otherness of Somerset. James's egg tempera paintings are pure-framed luminosity: of skies, these moors and rainbows, which for us in Somerset are magical. Sometimes we are even treated to a double rainbow!

Down at Burrowbridge other artists have studios looking at the Parrett: Jenny Graham is a minute from the water. She also captures the landscape in watercolour, oil and mixed media. One that stays in my mind is of the iconic Burrow Mump, so near, and from which you can see the Mendips which also inspire her. As I am sure do the myths, monuments and legends with which the

Isle of Athelney is awash, about the Great King Alfred, his retreat and battle here. But there is no myth about the village hall café at Burrowbridge where a group of villagers decided to organise a market some four years ago on the second Saturday in the month to help fund the repairs they needed for the hall. This has brought the village, divided by the River Parrett and the main Taunton to Cotswolds road, together. They meet in a utilitarian post-war building of 1953 marking the coronation, built when materials were still short. And Jenny was the lead artist with four A-level students in a recent project that depicts the moors wildlife painted on a backdrop for the stage.

With several tables of local food, the café itself has become the focus. Those who run this order their bacon from the Pitney Farm shop, the eggs are local and the tea and coffee is fair trade; the price is right and there is a view of the Mump. Amidst friendly chatter, breakfast is brought to the table and refills of coffee and tea are a welcome thought. Since they refurbished the hall with the funds they raised from the market and the collective breakfast, they can take the bookings, coming in thick and fast, and with their extension can put on stage performances. Which all goes to show what astonishing outcomes can be realised with shared goals, benefiting everyone, regardless of age. Each of these recent village markets have developed their own character and purpose with their own ingenuity, learning from each other of course, as they always did, but without any external interference. Walter Bagehot would have approved.

Chapter 6

The county town of Taunton

Wiveliscombe: a capital little township of the Brendons and Cothay Manor Gardens

Dulverton: Exmoor, romance and rivers

The county town of Taunton

*F*rom Burrowbridge you can follow, as I do sometimes, the old road that linked the west country with the Cotswolds, straight across the moors, where there are still signs of basketry. And there are market gardens where, if you are lucky, you can buy a cauliflower or a lettuce cut straight from the field behind a farmhouse that often has buckets of daffodils by the roadside in spring.

Absolutely none of these journeys requires time wasted in traffic jams on large main roads or motorways. And as Taunton is accessible by public transport from many central, south and west Somerset locations, this has to be the best way. Moreover as the town is low-lying a feast of church spires greets you when you approach by train.

The River Tone runs through the town, and there is a surprisingly large park, where the fishponds were nurtured for medieval kings and bishops. There are more splendid civic buildings, elegant terraces and churches than this essay can justify. Taunton, castle and all, has, undeniably the air of a county town.

Taunton's history concerns farming but also trade and manufacturing; there were cottage industries based on wool until the late eighteenth century and then, like Bruton, silk was woven here. Defoe was delighted to find 'eleven hundred looms going' in the 1720s.

Being near the seaports of Minehead and Watchet and *en route* to Lyme Regis, it became a staging post for these and for the east–west axis. Happily the fruit of the land and husbandry lives on at the cattle market and a new weekly Farmers' Market in the High Street, to which Charlton Orchards, dairies, beef producers, a trout farm and a baker from Devon, bring their produce.

Until the late seventeenth century, Taunton's history was peppered with violent episodes, centred around the castle. This was fought over and besieged during the Civil War, then followed uprising, and horrendous punishment. A time span of 1,000 years of conflict began with the Saxon King Ine, who built his fort on palisades. This was captured and destroyed in AD 772. After the Norman Conquest the castle was rebuilt on the same site, possibly by Henry de Blois, and became part of the extended land of the Bishops of Winchester. By 1490 it was ruined, repaired and then taken on behalf of the Cornish insurgents by Perkin Warbeck in 1497.

In 1577 Bishop Horne repaired it again, with only seventy years respite before the Civil War, when Parliament won it. The castle was regained by the Royalists only to be retaken by the Parliamentarians under Admiral Blake. Not surprisingly, when Charles II was restored he 'dismantled' the castle, which had harboured insurgents. He was not taking any chances with the west, but of course this was not the end. Once again, Taunton turned when it welcomed the Duke of Monmouth with open arms in 1685. The adulation here going to his head, he permitted the populace to proclaim him King in the market place. This history and the number of nonconformist chapels are evidence of both Taunton's and the county's strong independent character.

The bloody sequel is Somerset history with a capital H. A few miles away near Westonzoyland, the last battle on English soil took place, the Battle of Sedgemoor. Afterwards at the castle, Fairfax and Judge Jeffries, in their Bloody Assizes, inflicted their worst on all of the Duke of Monmouth's supporters in the west country. In 1822 the see of Winchester sold this pivotal building and it later became the home of the Somerset Archaeological and Natural History Society and the county museum. Now peace reigns over this river-hugging situation.

Diagonally-placed chimneys on Gray's Almshouses

The buildings that signify the long history of conflict and wealth, are not immediately obvious, but they are all here; for example Gray's Almshouses in East Street, an early example of Somerset brickwork. Here also in Mary Street, is one of the very first nonconformist chapels with which Taunton is well endowed. You can see the Castle Bow — the last surviving tower of the outer bailey, which had a drawbridge – from bus or car, and of course the slender, decorated tower of St Mary Magdalene at the end of the splendid Hammet Street of 1788. One finds all the pre-1700 buildings, both secular and religious, located within in a loose square shape, with the castle inside the early ditches.

One early spring, on a misty morning, after buying a picnic at the Farmers' Market, I decided to explore Vivary Park, which I had only seen during the flower show. The elegant park was laid out in 1894 beyond the town ditches, called Hurlditch and Townditch. Between a pair of ornate Victorian gates of 1876, past a war memorial designed by Ivor Shellard, I found fountains, rustic shelters and paths that spread out to a more natural area called Wilton lands. Soon it becomes apparent that something much larger had predated the Victorian park.

Although the site of the medieval vivarium had been covered over, the knowledge was not lost, hence the park's naming. In

1982 an excavation confirmed the position of the original stew-ponds, which had become silted. They covered some seventy acres and from 1207 eels and other fish, especially pike — a much revered dish — were kept to supply the household of the Manor of Taunton Dene at the castle.

Records reveal that before Christmas 1239 King Henry II ordered the royal angler, Hartaldus, and others, to catch 100 bream and forty pike for his hunting lodge at Woodstock. Furthermore he asked that the bream be baked in pastry, whilst thirty of the pike were salted and the rest preserved in gelatine. But it seems Henry's feasts were more famous for quantity than good taste: 'the quality of ale and food was so frightful that people dreaded attending' wrote Phillipa Pullar in her *Consuming Passions*. The four-day-old fish and hastily made bread and wine were so exceptionally unpalatable that, according to Peter de Blois, 'a man need close his eyes, and clench his teeth, wry-mouthed and shuddering, filtering this stuff rather than drinking'!

The leap from a medieval fish larder to the twentieth century is a long one. Above the ponds an eighteen-hole golf course was opened in 1928 near leisurely walks along brooks. Although once private, there has always been public access and in 1851 the first of the now famous flower shows took place. In 2004 a new chain swag and post fence for roses replaced the earlier design by Veitch of Exeter. One of the charming rustic shelters built around 1905 remains, the other is a successful copy. This neighbourhood of Taunton is civilised and encircled by terraces of stately Georgian houses with railings, giving them privacy, and their own park perspective.

I then explored the area of the Old Town and Wilton Gaol. This now houses the constabulary. It replaced the old lockup, under the Guildhall and House of Correction near the Tone Bridge. Altered in 1814 by George Pollard, it became the county gaol in 1841 and still has a forbidding central tower. Hereon there are examples of many architectural periods.

Across to Shuttern where the asymmetrical Shire Hall of 1855 was designed by the architect W.B. Moffat, George Gilbert Scott's former partner, with whom he worked on the Union Workhouses and County Asylum. It is a neo-Tudor design with a prominent porch and turret. And between the wars the county commissioned Vincent Harris, one of the most prolific civic architects of the decade, to design the County Hall near the Shire Hall.

For Georgian elegance see The Crescent of 1807, built by Sir Benjamin Hammet, one time keeper of the castle. At one end, at the same height as the houses, the Masonic Hall stands proudly with large Corinthian pilasters and pedimented entrance. I can guarantee that in most towns and cities the best town houses seem to be occupied by the legal profession. Brass name plates prove the point in The Crescent. However, the domestic character is kept with delightful fanlights, pretty first-floor balustrades, balconies and round-headed windows. More Georgian charm can be found in Bath Place, formerly Hunts Court. This was once enclosed; a narrow street, where double-fronted houses with gardens face a row of uniform, two-storied nineteenth-century shops — some with original windows and lovely hexagonal glazed fanlights. Bath Place is rightfully listed. You can shop at the fishmonger, or at the permanent home of the Country Market: buckets of cottage garden flowers sit outside; inside are all the home-made bakery and preserves we have come to expect. From the Makers Gallery you can choose from two showrooms of craft: furniture, jewellery, textiles and ceramics. And lose yourself over two floors at Brendon Books.

Hexagonal fanlights in Bath Place

One can imagine Taunton society making across Fore Street and North Street to place their orders at another shop that was founded in 1830. The County Stores is the only independent grocery store in the town, still family-owned, covering two floors and very much a meeting place. This would also have provided for Taunton's discerning residents in Hammet Street.

At the other end of town in Station Road there are two more independent shops in what was much later another stylish shopping street. One cannot miss Gurd's the gentleman's outfitters, still wearing late Victorian Art Nouveau tiles and faience on its façade — originally a chemist, and opposite this Stillman's, the famous, Somerset family-owned butcher who have helped and trained many others in the county.

Now for the castle, approached through Castle Bow, passing the Castle Hotel — a hotel since 1805 — and the County Museum – a museum where the building is as much of an exhibit as the collections it houses. In 1874 the Somerset Archaeological and Natural History Society bought the castle and began to install its collections with the help of public appeals — including enchanting-sounding 'calico balls' at the former Assembly Rooms, in 1870. The library houses a large collection relating to the natural history of the county. And nearby, some of their lectures are held in the Wyndham Hall, a small single-storey building of 1927, incorporating a large oak medieval doorway, rescued from Corporation Street.

Castle Green seems to cosset the buildings of the inner courtyard. These are three storeyed, embattled, and some of the south-facing windows, restored by Sir Benjamin Hammet in 1785, reflect the prevailing style of Strawberry Hill Gothic. This style is repeated in the south-west-facing tower, where the Society has its offices. One of the original sixteenth-century almshouses from St James Street has been reconstructed in front of the museum, making a contrast with its lime-washed and timber frame. Another fetching detail on the wall of what is called Castle House, where the curator lived at the beginning of the twentieth century, takes the eye — a fine, seventeenth-century plaster shell porch.

One cannot help having favourite objects in such a collection. Mine celebrates man's ingenuity in working with the elements over almost two millennia. The late prehistoric Shapwick canoe, six metres long and dated around 350 BC, was discovered 100 years ago when someone was cleaning a ditch near Shapwick. The Peat Moors Centre has its own replica. These vessels, constructed from one piece of oak, would have carried both people and goods, linking us with Meare. Another is on show in the Glastonbury Lake Museum, housed in the Tribunal.

Yet another water-related exhibit takes us back further to 2,900 BC — a section of a hurdle called the Walton trackway, found in 1975. Now it is black from the preserving medium of peat. It is sixty metres long, made of willow and hazel and its purpose was to save travellers from sinking into the peat. I stopped in my tracks, looking at an object almost 5,000 years old, whose construction does not differ from the hurdles that I have just had made for my own garden!

From the more recent late Bronze Age, a very fine round shield, found at South Cadbury in 1997, was donated by Mrs Montgomery, whose family we met in Chapter Three. This beautiful piece is made from 6,020 small bosses, each 4mm in diameter and individually stamped. It is thought that it had more of a ceremonial than confrontational use. Some of Somerset's Roman finds, such as jewellery and coins, are shown, as well as examples of Elton Ware from Clevedon and Donyatt pottery. A splendid Taunton cabinet, made for the Great Exhibition of 1851, designed to show the skills of the local craftsmen, is truly a 'museum piece' with intense inlaid floral decoration and carving achieving the objective.

Currently the museum has insufficient space to display much of its works on paper but their most recent acquisition, a watercolour of Cothelstone church by Edward Bawden, painted as recently as 1972, made my day. Other artists are shown in small exhibitions; one showed the work of Rachel Reckitt of Roadwater, whose sculpture we meet later, and another, Taunton artist Harry Frier who recorded many street traders, for example, the cockle and watercress seller, as well as a fine image of the castle.

This only scratches the surface of what engages me in Taunton and has in many cases been superbly researched elsewhere. However, I do believe Taunton needs a dedicated County Art Gallery so that the collections of Somerset's fine artistic past, as well as its phenomenal contemporary talent, have a permanent and wider audience. Let us hope the bid for new space by the Castle Museum will be successful and help to underpin the collecting policy that this county deserves.

Wiveliscombe: a capital little township of the Brendons and Cothay Manor Gardens

Wiveliscombe sits comfortably among the foothills of the Brendon Hills. These run from the sea, at the south-western edge of the Quantocks, to Exmoor. The Brendons have less of the chocolate box about them than Holford in the Quantocks; they are less bleak than the unpeopled parts of Exmoor. Nevertheless their beautiful churches and farmhouses prepare you for Exmoor. If the fairly solitary road from Watchet across the hills to Wiveliscombe is taken, these character changes emerge, gently.

Travelling from the east, however, gives one the rich experience of the Vale of Taunton Deane. For centuries this was in the vanguard of agricultural progress and called 'the paradise of England'. It is still as fruitful as Thomas Fuller found in the mid-1600s: 'to use their [the peasants] phrase with Zun and Zoil alone, that it needs no manuring'; indeed those peasants asked, wasn't 'Tonton Deane' the only place to be born?

Off the main road, and the bus does a nice little diversion through Milverton, just before Wiveliscombe, a compact, prosperous-looking village with cobbled paths and charming architecture. This grew as rich on wool as its close neighbour; it has a church (that holds good concerts), many artists and an annual street fair in May, where everything from local art to local food is widely available.

But Wiveliscombe itself is a town that has served well those who have lived and farmed among the hills for 600 years. Like Watchet, it has grappled with and succumbed to many invaders: the Romans, the Saxons, the Vikings, who availed themselves of the cattle, and of course the Normans. Nothing remains of the palace built by, and a favourite seat of, Bishop John de Drokensford, where at least one Archbishop of Canterbury 'kept his birthday' in 1331. And a manor house built on the site in 1735 was destroyed by fire fifty years ago.

In its medieval prime, the town supported two weekly markets. One, held on Saturday, was still active when John Collinson, the vicar of Long Ashton, published his volumes of Somerset history. He recorded a market house — where tithes from the sale of wool were collected and received by Bishop Bull in 1559 — a shambles and three annual fairs, for sheep, cattle and 'pedlary' — implements and iron wares. The fairs took place at the beginning of May, Trinity Monday and 25 September. This number signifies the little town's success between 1550 and 1750 when cloth and blankets were woven as well as carolinas. These were felt hats, chiefly made from rabbit fur, considered to be 'a course [sic] mean commodity' in 1702.

By 1750 the wool market had changed: prices had fallen, but strong characters and family businesses came to the rescue. We can see evidence of the success of one particular family at the Court House in the Square. It makes more of an impression than the Market Hall of 1806, which formerly had a portico. The Court House was remodelled in 1881 and much embellished by the Hancock family, who owned the brewery. This is a delightful example of the Victorian love affair with the 'Elizabethan'. Except for the reading room, which was built in the same style in 1877, this style is without precedent in the town itself. It is tile-hung with elaborately carved jetties that may have come from another building. The grand staircase and beautiful handrail remind me, now that the shop sells materials and furniture, of the Liberty store in London, where we bought our dress materials and furnishings in the 1960s.

In its relatively short life the Court House has played several parts: as a department store in the 1930s, as a bank and, interestingly for me, having traced others, it served as a British Restaurant during the Second World War. These public restaurants were set up all over the country, frequently in fine buildings, backed by design blueprints from the government itself. The purpose was to serve all comers a two-course lunch at a very reasonable price. However, this one is unique because Sir Alfred Munnings, one-time president of the Royal Academy, recorded its transient existence for posterity. In his cartoon advertising a whist drive, the tongue in cheek representation of 1943, is a far cry from his formal portraits of riders and their horses or his depictions of Exmoor in tranquil mood; with herds of ponies by water. He lived at Withypool between 1940 and 1945 and would have visited the Hancock family.

Wiveliscombe doorway

Wiveliscombe is not short of elegant town houses: one side of Town Hill is graced with a terrace with generous Georgian windows and once you start to explore there are any number of much older houses, some medieval — look out for what is thought to be the oldest timber-framed and stone cottage, called The Old House, and an interesting passage with the numerals 1804 applied in wood, in stunning figures over the six-panelled door.

Mr Charles Lukey Collard, a member of a local family, having set up a business making pianos in London, also wanted a country residence in Somerset for entertaining. Like those featured in Mark Girouard's *The Victorian Country House*, Abbotsfield reflects the later-nineteenth century's growing consumerism. Smaller than average, it was designed in 1872 by Owen Jones, an eminent Victorian architect, towards the end of his life. Jones's work on the interior of the Great Exhibition is widely celebrated and studied because the commissions were colour-matched schemes, which promoted his thesis that in all great work, only the primary colours should be employed; just as stylised repetitive patterns were his leitmotif. (As far as I know his only west country work is St Bartholomew at Sutton Waldron in Dorset.)

The asymmetrical design promises the attributes of the Victorian gentleman's country house: a large orangery — very fashionable — a chamfered tower, projecting gables, a music (later called ball) room and a picture room. The house was located and designed to take advantage of exceptional views — evidently of Glastonbury Tor. There were ample servants' quarters and the stabling required for the smooth running and entertaining that such a house demanded. However with a mix of styles, the stature and potential were not fully realised. Would a disagreement between the clients and the artist explain this? Four years later the house was offered for sale and Mrs Collard, reputedly not liking the house, returned to Bournemouth — their other country house. However Mr Collard did not sell and held concerts here; it is said that Richard Wagner and Dame Addelina Patti might have performed for his guests. Today it has been sensitively converted into apartments.

The recently published and very well-researched book of Wiveliscombe compiled by the Wiveliscombe book group, illustrates the ballroom and staircase, both with classical features, together with some lively memories of those who worked there below stairs.

St Andrew's parish church has stature. It was rebuilt in sandstone by Richard Carver in 1829, leaving little of the earlier periods to see. It is surprisingly spacious, with a mood that reflects the Georgian rather than the later high Victorian Gothic. Among the restrained but elegant decoration, there are boxed pews and a west gallery with Carver's name, unusually, signed in gilt lettering. The piers of the five bays are 'modelled on the Somerset perp standard'. His other local works are at Bridgwater and he enlarged Over Stowey eleven years later and Holy Trinity in Taunton. I noted that there is a regular programme of music and suspect that the acoustics here are very good.

There are also two nonconformist chapels. One is now an art gallery and meeting space where local lectures are held. And at Waterrow a group of artists have individual studios at Hurstone Farm. Louise Waugh, whose vibrant landscapes are familiar, is exhibiting here in Somerset Art Weeks and now lives in Wiveliscombe, but she is not alone: 'Wivey' seems to be awash with talent: seen for example in its public art in the Jubilee garden, where there are some contemporary metal gates.

More down to earth maybe, but I think Wivey's outdoor swimming pool speaks volumes. Sitting here on a warm summer evening, when both children and adults enjoy the water, is like being in a time capsule of Somerset frolics and 'streets-aheadness'. This was built in 1927, ten years before Greenbank at Street, as a town memorial — together with the recreation ground — to local soldiers lost in the First World War. What an enlightened and sustaining idea. It was the first public open-air pool in Somerset and is still run by the town for the town, with what I thought were few, but the obvious, constraints.

Just one year earlier Walter Wilkinson came to Wiveliscombe with his peep or puppet show — we meet him retired at Selworthy.

He remembered the town with fondness; for the vegetable shop, the landscape and because his performance in the square won the praise of one elderly chap who told him 'you gie I the best larf I 'ad in many a year'.

Today I feel he would be just as pleased to find the Wivey larder with fresh local vegetables, a good butcher, pharmacy, library, stationers, an emporium selling all needs for the horse and country person, as well as Court House. And after a gap of some twenty-odd years, brewing has been brought back to Wiveliscombe with not one, but now two breweries; the Cotleigh and the Exmoor! Again, Wivey excels. Just a few years after Wilkinson, garages came to Wiveliscombe. Mr Leonard Jones, an engineer opened his in 1936 and the original lettering which is phosphorous bronze, his grandson told me — never needs polishing. Seventy this year and still going.

Wiveliscombe must have one of the largest number of societies, groups, clubs and organisations of any small Somerset town. With every age, need, interest, inclination and pursuit being catered for, it really surpasses many towns twice this size. Wiveliscombe has a strong and palpable sense of community, being the sort of town where people look out for one another and where if you miss the bus someone will give you a lift!

Taunton to Wivey by bus is easy, but you might need a car to reach the hidden Cothay Manor Gardens in the Tone Valley, although it is not far from the West Deane Way. Cothay is a rare, embattled, fifteenth-century manor house found among deep-cut, winding lanes, red-washed by west Somerset rain. But the rain brings forth wild pink foxgloves on every verge in May and June.

Cothay Manor and contemporary gardens

One wonders how it was possible to improve upon the beautiful bone structure of the garden. But Mr and Mrs Robb have done so dramatically, in their recreation of a garden, first laid out in the 1920s. They have employed symmetry with playfulness all the more apparent, in such a romantic and picturesque context. This is a garden to see in high summer when it is ablaze. June is the month.

The red stone, two-storeyed manor house is reflected in water. Ducklings cavort among the lily pads. Behind the house, terraces, fulsome borders and yew hedges mingle with ravishing planting and beyond the new lake there are meadows. The flower gardens face west towards the river. Separated from the terraces and herbaceous borders, they are enclosed as garden rooms by the yew, which provides cool corridors between flashes of colour and height. These *allées* are punctuated by large, stone pots overflowing with at least fifty different species of flowers.

In the Bishop's garden the parterre is box and the colour theme is red; with the divine papaver 'Patty's Plum', *Knautia macedonia*, phormium, *Heuchura* 'Palace Purple' and deep maroon sweet peas. In the herbaceous border, the delphiniums run from deep inky blue to white, mingled with foxgloves, alstromeria and *Francoa sanchifolia*, its tall spires of unassuming pink buds giving little indication of the forthcoming petit point-like petals. Even more height is achieved in with the creamy flowers of *Crambe cordifolia* and yellow cephalaria.

There is ingenuity and pleasing proportion in the avenue of the unicorn where grafted, mop-headed robinia seem to sail above billowing, lilac nepeta, whose rounded habit repeats the shape of the trees. Between the planted areas, and under arches to the grotto garden, where plants spring up from the paths, the yew creates a sense of surprise. And the shears have been used to advantage in the topiary. The walk leads through a walled area, past the nursery and glasshouses to a meadow, where an apple tree's misshapen boughs bend groundwards with age. No formal shaping here; rather an oasis surrounded by pines in which one can enjoy a simple homemade tea served from a small building, covered with roses.

The fascinating manor house is the backdrop. You can see the transomed windows and buttressing from the garden. Mr and Mrs Robb are delighted to show small, pre-booked, parties their home. The tour includes the chapel, with its unusual gallery for servants, the timber ceilings, turret stairs and fifteenth-century wall paintings — among the earliest remaining in an English house.

Dulverton: Exmoor, romance and rivers

Just mentioning Dulverton may be enough to summon up a store of images and memories, because of its associations with the novel *Lorna Doone* by R.D. Blackmore. But Dulverton is real, an all-year-round town; it is as E.F. Delderfield wrote 'the only place with any pretension of being a town on the moor itself'.

Travelling from Wiveliscombe another bus route teasingly takes a foray into Devon at Bampton. But one wintry morning I took the moorland bus from Dunster to Dulverton. I was one of two passengers, and the journey was one of the loveliest in Somerset. Only on the bus or in a saddle can you see over the hedges and look down at the River Exe as it tumbles south, a shining blend of wood and water. This is one of the introductions to Dulverton. The river curves and twists on its journey to Devon, having begun in the wilderness-like terrain of the Chains, high on the moor. Climbing Dunkery is another rite of passage for which my first Exmoor boots have survived the test of time. I wondered how I did it, and in the snow, one Easter?

Autumn in this Exe Valley is enclosed, lush green before turning gold. In winter there is more sky through bare, brown branches and red wands of cornus. Ivy leaves gleam where they hug the tree trunks, roads are lace-edged with the remains of the coppery beech and bracken papers the rising hills. This road was traffickless, except for a rider. Reading R.D. Blackmore later I saw how the author uses the character of Jan Ridd to express his own love of nature and Exmoor. And if we listen to the silence we can also hear, as Ridd remarks 'the gentle tinkle of the stream ... louder than my doings'.

This road never loses touch with water from three different rivers. First it follows the Avil just outside Dunster, after Timberscombe a steep climb to the Rest and Be Thankful Inn at Wheddon Cross, and a snowdrop valley to see in February. Before long the Quarme flows in from the west, and at Coppleham the Exe joins. At Bridgetown we almost collided with a weir; the water gains pace, and on the right there is a thatched cricket pavilion, perched in a corner. Here James Horrobin the blacksmith lived as a child, and here, he could lean out and look at the cricket pitch. He also told me of his first job, polishing boots taught by the butler of Mr Nesfield, the land agent at that time.

As the road drops, the banks become moss covered, but the beech leaves were holding on. At Helebridge we leave the avenue of trees, where a little to the south the Exe meets the Barle.

What a difference 200 years can make! Taking the same journey in 1808, William Gilpin, who could picture the picturesque for England, agreed, but only for the first six miles, finding 'the hills with their woody skirts to the road'. But not later: the 'woody hills became dreary slopes, cut into portions, by naked hedges, unadorned by a single tree'. Not now.

Dulverton once had two railway lines, in those steam days – to Barnstaple on the Taunton line and to Exeter on the Exe Valley line, where the twelve stops included seven halts, making most villages and hamlets accessible. Coinciding with the railways was the building in 1873 of the Caernarvon Arms, a fashionable anglers hotel, one of the earliest purpose-built hotels in the region. And yes it is now converted, but it was known throughout the world, and even mentioned in an angling article in the *New York Times*. Were the salmon and trout as plentiful, I wondered, as those I saw once at the Waterville Inn in the Ring of Kerry? Later on the banks of the Barle I did, reassuringly, see some anglers.

Looking at Dulverton today it is difficult to believe that this was an industrial town. There were four mills driven by the leat that begins and ends at the River Barle: a paper mill, a grist mill, a woollen mill that became a crepe mill, as well as another, now residential, Mill House. Fifty-five years ago the department store belonging to Thornes attracted a large crowd of bargain-hunters when they closed; now divided, but both halves still sell clothes. A hardware shop has taken over from the ironmonger of Fore Street — W. & L. German, established in 1847 — who advertised their sole agency for Nobel's ballistic ammunition. Could I make a tenuous socio-historical link with the funding of literature, among other Nobel prizes — by the manufacture of arms — and John Steinbeck whom we met in Chapter Three? Dulverton-born John L. German, brother or partner of the above, was a professional photographer and his picture of the feast commemorating Queen Victoria's diamond jubilee of 1887 shows Bank Square filled to the gunwales with top-hatted and flat-capped gentlemen, ladies with straw hats, banners and tables covered with food. Beef would surely have been served, as it often was at such feasts, along with plum pudding, even in high summer!

The family firm of Gerald David has another branch in Dulverton, naturally selling local and Exmoor beef. Whilst Rothwell and Dunworth the antiquarian bookshop, established for twenty-five years, is an absolute gem. Original windows pull you in and there are two floors. All the better to browse among. And the Dulverton laundry, established for nearly a century, still does a good

The Bookshop

trade with other hotels in spite of the demise of the Caernarvon Arms.

As the town is in a bowl, the hills are present from any point or corner: from outside Sydenham Hall, the former house of the Sydenhams of Combe Sydenham, or in Fore Street, from the churchyard and indeed looking down past what was once the Lamb as well as from the Lion, with a crouching namesake. As one would expect, together with the inns there are several successful teashops and a delicatessen. And chatting over a cup of coffee in the Lion I found myself talking to the very lady who once used to climb up and clean the Lamb above the now defunct inn!

Dulverton, to a lesser degree than Exford, hosted the meets for Dulverton Staghounds in the Market Square, and this space came into its own with the filming of *Land Girls* in 1998; full of people cheering, with the flying steps added to the Market House in 1927, seen to their best advantage. Originally built in 1760, and altered in the nineteenth century, the later steps sail up either side of an arch to an elegant half-glazed porch and podium. They were designed by Sir Albert Richardson, a friend of the Herbert family of nearby Pixton Park, where his first design, I was told by Mrs Herbert's granddaughter, was a garden house. Sir Albert, later made president of the Royal Academy, makes a further contribution to Dulverton with the Catholic church, below.

I found far less red sandstone in Dulverton than in any of the other west Somerset villages. Here stone is darker, more Devonian, although you can also see where cob was used, and later, in the nineteenth and twentieth centuries, it was brick. All Saints' church is sandstone however, with a sturdy thirteenth-century tower, befitting the town, above. On the cold February day when I visited grass and snowdrops had a fine coverlet of snow. Unlike Dunster, this was restored in 1855 by Edward Ashworth of Exeter, leaving little of the earlier features, except part of a fifteenth-century rood screen.

The life of a local visionary, George Williams born at Ashway Farm and known all over the world as founder of the YMCA, is celebrated with a stained-glass window. And just after Williams's birth the Poor Law Reform Act was passed, giving each area the power to re-institute the workhouses, thus another kind of public philanthropy resulted in the large, but secular building in the same year as the restoration of All Saints. It was the new Dulverton Union or workhouse, also designed by Ashworth. History always has its darker side and nowhere is it more grim than in the details taken for the 1881 census. Listed among the fifty inmates, were a single mother with daughters of seven months and four years; a widowed father with two sons under twelve; and coincidentally, another single mother with two children called Blackmore, rather like the novelist. In all these post-Poor Law Reform Act unions the sexes were divided and a T-shaped building enabled each wing to provide for this segregation. Down by the bridge this imposing building with a central pediment and classical porch now houses a happier enterprise — the headquarters of Exmoor National Park.

Crossing back to Bridge Street, have a look at the crepe mill in Milhams Lane, housing the long-established laundry. There is a Congregational church of 1844, with its lancet windows stark against the white-rendered exterior. However, the church with the most colourful beginnings is that of St Stanislaus. How this came about makes an interesting story.

In 1944, at Pixton Park, a visiting priest converted an old corrugated laundry into a chapel for the Herberts — called the 'iron room' by the family. It served both the family and the scattered, moorland Catholic congregation. Ten years later Mrs Herbert persuaded Sir Albert to design a new church. The site was an old stable off the High Street in the town, and from the outset the whole project is one of donation and dedication.

The timber came from the grounds of the Park, the building was completed with voluntary labour and many of the interior furnishings were given: the altar crucifix by Eric Gill and original sanctuary lamp came from the Pixton Park chapel. Sir Mark Lennox Boyd donated a statue by Septimus Waugh of St George, carved from fumed chestnut; the chairs were made just over the border in Devon. Furthermore some of the recent stained-glass was made in Somerset by Chinks Grylls, who lives in Nether Stowey.

As Father Miller hinted, I found the space to be totally enveloping. I did not turn on the lights and the posts and rafters became a metaphor for woodland. The small round windows allow the light to filter through, just as trees do. Its scale suits the town, for this is an intimate place with its courts and alleys. Mrs Rothwell of the bookshop told me one of her first memories was of arriving in the war and being pushed around the town in her pram. She was overjoyed at the number of stables out of which so many horses poked their heads. As befitting a church which was once a stable, there is little decoration except for the round stained-glass windows and projecting entrance porch, white-rendered, wide-eaved, with a Voysey-ish air. The interior is all wood, and one of the paintings — a narrative of the Baptism of Christ — by Richard Rothwell, Mrs Rothwell's husband, was painted in the 1970s for the Baptistry. The connection between the Herbert family and the naming of the church came about through Mrs Herbert's son, who fought for the Polish army in the Second World War and then later helped to resettle the soldiers who could not return to Poland.

Now peaceful, Dulverton itself did not suffer as much as Lynton and Lynmouth from the floods of 15 August 1952; but a wooden sign near the bridge marks the high watermark of that fateful evening reminding us of man's fragile control over nature.

Chapter 7

The road west to the Quantocks, Nether Stowey and Kilve

Williton, Orchard Wyndham and the Bakelite Museum

Watchet: creative currents at a seaside town

Dunster: the castle and village

Illustration on previous page: The harbour at Watchet

The road west to the Quantocks, Nether Stowey and Kilve

*F*ollowing the theme of travelling west, to reach the Quantocks, from say Street, we keep to the Polden Hills for riverside Bridgwater, which connects with Taunton by rail. But for drama, the road up and over the width of the Quantock Hills from Crowcombe tumbling down into the old centre of Stowey must win.

Old Bridgwater is all brick and tiles, and has a museum celebrating the materials once made here. But just on the western outskirts there is a tone change. Seeing just one or two buildings in the deep Quantock red stone, heralds, for me, the beginning of west Somerset. Even before Bridgwater's nineteenth-century industrial growth, brick was used for some supremely elegant town houses. Among several, built by the Duke of Chandos around 1723, are those in Castle Street, originally named after him, where the elevations are a paradigm of the classical language of architecture. Two of the houses, first number 11 and now 13, are the Georgian home of the very first Arts Centre to be opened in the United Kingdom on 10 October 1946. One local 'enlightened patron of arts', Gwen Pollard, persuaded the Arts Council to support this.

Now, Nether Stowey itself is quiet, but you might imagine, as you stand outside Coleridge's cottage in Lime Street, that holiday-makers from Bridgwater and Bristol, perhaps in charabancs, would pass on their way to such destinations as Lynton and Minehead. In spite of the bypass which avoids this, and separates the village from the church, the village has seen little change in the last seventy-odd years. Nor has it grown much since I first walked the Quantock Hills and stayed at the foot of Holford Combe. Water still runs down the gullies of Castle Street, which forms one leg of the Y-shaped village pattern; although slightly diverted for the newer houses, the attractive cobbles in the pavement, surely from Kilve, are intact and the mixture of fine houses, cottages, and shops are alive.

Nether Stowey is a Quantock Hills gateway with endless walks. And numerous historical and cultural connections can be made from the Norman castle to twentieth-century literary associations. In the 1790s there were a series of encounters between a local man, Tom Poole, and many writers and poets, philosophers and inventors. It is not just the genius of Samuel Taylor Coleridge with which the village is synonymous, but also with William and Dorothy Wordsworth, Humphry Davy the chemist and physicist, Robert Southey, William Hazlitt, the brilliant critical essayist and Thomas de Quincy.

If any of these luminaries returned they would certainly recognise the central core. St Mary's Street has not changed, even the principle village shop, where butter was once made in their dairy, has been owned by the same family for some seventy years. Moreover Gulliford's, the garage on the other side, which opened in the same decade — in the same family, in an elegant house, for fifty years – is much the same. Their office still has the finest mahogany fittings I have seen, used to store car manuals! The fuel is still dispensed from some rarely seen, street pumps, and, as this is one of the few independents, it needs us. At the top of Castle Street there is a useful little library next to the Quantock Hills ranger's office, and Lime Street has a butcher.

Among several fine houses is the Old House, to which Tom Poole moved in 1802, after Coleridge left for the lakes. It has attractive late eighteenth-century glazing bars. Further east there is the half-hexagonal Toll House built in Quantock stone. There are Victorian and Georgian houses but also many others that are older. If one looks carefully at the doors and roofs in both Lime and Castle Streets one sees medieval examples, with timber jetties in Castle Street. Perhaps these housed the weavers who were making textiles at this time. Much later in the year 1897, Queen Victoria's Golden Jubilee, a clock tower with a wooden lantern was erected — also in Quantock stone — replacing an eighteenth-century market cross, where markets were held.

The gazebo at Stowey Court

Nether Stowey, near shaded combes, copses and 'fern-hung lanes', also has an interesting early history. The Domesday record mentions it being held by Alfred of Spain. A borough may have developed from the Norman castle, which was captured later in 1139 — the castle mound is located at the top of Castle Street. And St Mary's, which produced two bishops, has, on the north side, the delightful landmark at Stowey Court, a stately eighteenth-century garden gazebo.

But it is with books and writing that many associate Stowey. Later than the Romantics, Walter Raymond, the Somerset folk writer, who was a great friend of the Clark family, moved here from Withypool in 1921. He took an interest in many of the village doings and celebrations and lived at the large house of West Court, now Stowey Court Farm. Raymond enjoyed working in his garden, growing vegetables for himself and giving or selling them to friends. And it was in the same year that he began to make his study of children's songs (he knew Cecil Sharp, of course). According to Mrs Stacy of Little's Stores, the fame of Mr Moore's shire horses, which Raymond would have seen, pulling the wagons made in the village in Lime Street, is still a talking point.

Raymond saw the Women's Friendly Society walk to the

church and back to the Rose and Crown for tea, as they carried posies, also seen by Coleridge and possibly the oldest society of this kind for women in Somerset. Raymond would have talked to the Broom Squire. In her *Somerset Journal*, Berta Lawrence has a photograph of the Quantock Broom Squire, taken around 1950, carrying his birch brooms, one over each shoulder, each bound tight with willow or blackberry, in five tight cross-bands. He made these in Five Lords Combe with handles of oak or ash and the birch, cut in spring before it budded. He was the last of his tribe and lived at the Broom Squire's cottage until 1952, at Bincombe near Over Stowey. This started out as a hovel in 1639 and in the 1930s the Heal family (of furniture fame) used it as a holiday cottage. The current owners are immensely proud of this history. Anyone searching for stained glass designed by Burne-Jones should visit Over Stowey church

As Raymond perpetuated vernacular Somerset in his writing in the 1900s, so 100 years earlier, a local man, an authority on the practical details of tanning and agriculture, became the catalyst for the exciting period of English Romantic literature. Tom Poole was a self-educated man who had his own library and read works that included Tom Paine's *Rights of Man* and Mary Wollstonecraft's *Rights of Women*. De Quincy described Poole as 'a bachelor in a rustic old-fashioned house, simply furnished with modern luxuries'. His Castle Street house, once separated from the Coleridge's cottage by an orchard, is also Georgian with a splendid seven-bay façade with the Bark House or tanyard, where Quantock oaks were used in the leather-dressing process, nearby.

With Coleridge financially pressed in 1797 and needing a home for his young family, Poole found the poet a cottage where he could live 'among the simplicity of peasants'. Poole was unconventional by the standards of local rural society, neither wearing a wig nor powdering his hair — and was branded a rebel. But it was his dedication to liberal causes and his love of books that attracted Coleridge, not the unconventionality. For Poole's part, the attraction was Coleridge's scholarship, his elegant speech and ideas.

Notwithstanding our present-day fascination, the villagers must have been baffled by the arrival of these visionary romantics. They must have wondered what they were doing and why they came to this small village; in Coleridge's case from Bristol. Fortunately they did and Coleridge Cottage — now owned by the National Trust — where he lived for three years, gives us some of the material background to the poet's most prolific period. When Coleridge and his family lived here it was cramped and damp; he could not bring himself to destroy the mice, which were unwelcome visitors. Now it is clean, neat and habitable, the stairs are remade and the rooms are furnished with small pieces and portraits of the poets and their associations.

Through William Hazlitt's graphic pen-portraits we gain something of the differing characteristics of Coleridge and Wordsworth, their appearance and the landscape inspiration for their work. Wordsworth and his sister, encouraged by Coleridge, came to Holford nearby and rented Alfoxden Park. Both poets, sometimes accompanied by Dorothy Wordsworth, often composed as they walked, using notebooks to record their observations. One of Coleridge's poems encapsulates a quintessential village atmosphere with 'All the numberless goings on of life, Inaudible as dreams!'

Many of his most famous works — *Christabel, Frost at Midnight, The Rime of the Ancient Mariner* — as well as the *Lyrical Ballads*, written with Wordsworth, began here where he was as much concerned with the war with France as with changing society and scientific discoveries. The poetical connections continue as the present custodian publishes contemporary poetry. For those who want to tread in some of Coleridge's footsteps, a long-distance way from Nether Stowey to Porlock has been named after him — the Coleridge Way.

Nether Stowey has not suffered the same fate as Grasmere, the poet's next home. There are few camera-toting tourists here, but there is another artistic reason to visit, as well as the open studios in Somerset Art Weeks this year and biannually. Three times a year the Court Gallery in Castle Street hang changing exhibitions of nineteenth and twentieth-century British work, all beautifully mounted. I have seen work by Garnet Wolseley of the Newlyn School, whose pictures of his own children on the beach in Cornwall are light-filled, and who lived for over twenty years at the end of his life at Nettlecombe Court, near Roadwater.

Inspiration can still be found at Kilve beach, to which the poets walked the five miles or so. The lane to the beach passes the limestone church, a ruined chantry and a ruined brick chimney where an experiment to refine oil from shale was conducted in the 1920s. It is one of the few beaches without modern encroachment. Just the sight of children bent double over rock pools, crabbing or looking for fossils, brings one closer to a Wolseley picture or a Laura Knight, who was godmother to the Wolseley children.

For Kilve is all stone and dangerous to over-adventurous walkers when the tide is coming in! When blustery, I have seen the surfers standing by for rollers, black clad, with their surf boards held high, looking more fish-like than human. The rest of us are happy to sit and wonder at the strata, the many shades of stone, from almost coal black to the palest dove grey. The walk from 'Kilve's delightful shore', climbing to East Quantoxhead to see the church, Court House, the typical west Somerset round pillared barns and village with its duck pond, is perfect. A walk that could be timed to coincide with the days when Sir Walter and Lady Luttrell open their garden at the Court.

But perhaps tea first at Chantry Tea Gardens at Kilve — picturesque but not pretentious. It has ruins on two sides and the seats are set out among sedum and hollyhocks, hens and sparrows. If wedges of cake or scones and cream fit your bill, they are baked here. It doesn't matter what time you arrive and there is hot soup in the winter. Chantry Cottage is on the Luttrell estate and the ruined chantry has attracted its share of stories: some must be true, others may be village myth. Supposedly smugglers used the ruins in the eighteenth century to hide casks of liquor; it appears that when the smugglers heard that the excise men had arrived, the rapid retreat resulted in a fire and this is how it became ruinous.

Further clever timing could mean that walking at the end of a summer afternoon, as the sun goes down, gives you the chance to see one of the superb flame-streaked coastal sunsets. I am always loath to leave this location.

Williton, Orchard Wyndham, and the Bakelite Museum

From Kilve to Williton, the walled road curves like *a route en corniche,* with the sea below the hill of West Quantoxhead. Then a heavenly experience downhill where, although the traffic winds through, Williton shrugs its shoulders and carries on as it always has, in true Somersetshire fashion.

The poet Edward Thomas wrote *In Pursuit of Spring* in 1914 describing a cycle journey he made from London to the Quantocks. He also found this combination of hills and sea, passing St Audries, which was the prelude to his arrival in Williton, utterly beautiful. He wrote: 'to the fact that it [Williton] was on the main road from Minehead to Bridgwater it was as indifferent as to the marriage of heaven and earth'.

In truth Williton should be less reticent about what it offers. As the farmer with whom I stay at West Quantoxhead says 'you can find everything you need in Williton'; great for hard-pressed farmers, who need their machinery working when the weather is right and travellers alike. In the large agricultural, gardening and outdoor shop of Gliddons, walkers searching for a small knapsack, or gardeners in need of overshoes, will strike lucky. In the one main street there is a baker and a large independent grocer — the County Stores, now the only branch besides Taunton. Williton has a butcher, who also sells fish and cheese, and a wonderfully large greengrocer's shop. This is run by the same family who, since the railway opened, have had the right, for ten shillings, to sell ripe fruit at Williton railway station. The Victorians were often there first!

Yes, Williton has a station: one of the dearly cared-for ones on the West Somerset Railway to Watchet, Dunster and Minehead, where each waiting room has been restored to reflect a particular decade.

West Somerset Railway

Here the idea was to recreate the late 1940s and it is worth seeing the other facilities! Their re-ordering fits well with another reason to go to Williton — the Bakelite Museum.

Williton has the only original and working signal box from what was the Bristol and Exeter railway. At the kiosk you are given one of those proper card tickets named after Edmondson, the gentleman who invented the machine that punched them out. The service is faultless, the uniforms are impeccable – as is the stationmaster who wears a buttonhole. Whilst the lady who serves tea is eager for you to try her homemade sponge cake. And it was good. Even a wintry day finds the volunteers, who run the whole line professionally, painting the platform and its GWR seats ready for the next season. Flowers are planted, parking is free and the maze in the crossing keeper's cottage is just the kind of railway oddity we need.

It was to this station that the large orders of fruit and vegetables were sent from Covent Garden for Orchard Wyndham, the manor house of the nearby Wyndham estate. In a fruit and vegetable book of 1871, small, leather, fitted with a clasp and elegantly inscribed on headed estate paper, I read the details, dates and quantities. In February one order included currants, gooseberries and lettuce and another included 8lb of seakale, a very fashionable Victorian dish. To discover how this delicate vegetable should be grown Dorothy Hartley gives an illustration in her pioneering *Food in England*; it should be grown next to a wall, on seaweed, with stones and gravel on top, no earth should soil the prized, blanched shoots. It was served like asparagus with butter, as a separate dish.

Butter was, of course, made in large quantities on all farms and estates — as I found in the butter books for the Wyndham's Silverton Park Estate in Devon. Butter would also have been made on the home farm at Orchard Wyndham. In 1884 between 3 and 7lbs were made on any given day and the surplus was sold; between June and September 85lbs were made and 59lbs sold. For Orchard Wyndham, the bread orders were written in a looser hand than the other accounts. Perhaps the cook or kitchen maid, rather than the housekeeper, was responsible. But both bills and bread orders were always made up to the quarter day — from Lady Day to Midsummer and so on. Horner's stores in Williton supplied the flour, but items such as Pear's soap, cotton binding, starch and matches came from Gliddons; wine from Joseph Trance, ordered in a gold embossed book; and what most fascinated me was the first entry for petroleum supplied by Gliddons, sold in a two-gallon can for 1/8d in 1900. As garages did not exist at the turn of that century ironmongers and others began to sell fuel, but only in cans.

The manor house and estate of Orchard Wyndham, south-west of Williton, has been in the Orchard and later the Wyndham families since the thirteenth-century. It is in a felicitous position, near water, among a circle of hills with marvellous views.

From the park, the roofline of this puzzling house resembles a small hamlet, with its Tudor chimneys. It was originally early medieval, then enlarged through successive centuries: firstly in the Tudor period, again after the Restoration, and it was embellished in the early eighteenth century. The late Dr Katherine Wyndham and Richard Haslam, in their article for *Country Life*, quote from John Gay writing to Alexander Pope in 1732, who praised the 'real improvements' and many 'visionary castles' — follies, perhaps — added by Sir William Wyndham. Sir William also built an amphitheatre and held sports for his neighbours. Could his inspiration have been Vanbrugh's work at Claremont Landscape Garden in Surrey, which I know well? In this garden the architect Vanbrugh conceived the Belvedere for entertainment, where the game of hazard was played and where there is also a famous amphitheatre, built between 1715 and 1729.

The development of the house is complicated. The original E-shape was built around a courtyard with a small hall with some of the Tudor additions. Having been pulled down, only the north front survives from that period. However by looking at the outside it is possible to see where the later work on the elevations took place. Sir John Wyndham, who made this his home in 1530, made the greatest changes.

What singles out this garden is the location and aspect: one can see where there was a wing of an earlier house and the sloping hills to the west provide a view that betters anything any of us could usually hope to see. A walled lake, avenues of superb specimen trees and, for me, the whole picture is completed by the rich sandstone farmhouse ranges: stables, barns and stores, some enclosed on three sides with cobbled yards, built against the weather. Here too is one of the first icehouses, of 1530, which towers above the lower drive. I look forward to seeing the great hall, and some of the ten rooms that are shown with some fine furniture and paintings, during the summer.

This pastoral theme continues at the ultimate and unexpected delight of Orchard Mill, housing the extraordinary Bakelite Museum. This family-run museum is unfettered by attendants or turnstiles. Orchard Mill, across fields, near a river called Stream, contains a collection virtually dedicated to consumerism and the twentieth century. Could there be a more incongruous setting for the history of plastic and the largest collection of Bakelite in the world?

I shall always remember my first meeting with this collection. I arrived at half past six, after one of my long field days, but my late arrival did not diminish the welcome, completed by a makeshift tea. My contribution was inevitably some cheese I had bought earlier, shared with the curator and owner Patrick Cook and his young daughter.

On the grass approach there is a 1930s brown and cream caravan by Bertram Hutchins of Winchester, fitted with modern comforts and Tudorbethan wood interior, and the obligatory picnic basket. Together with the first plastic bike and old farm machinery, these set the pace – transporting visitors into a world of leisurely picnics and charabanc excursions. Here also is the prototype for Patrick's latest design called the Pod: sleek, swept back, based on a 1950s caravan and putting up two rather nicely. Patrick, a trained sculptor, started his plastics collection at Greenwich in 1974. Bakelite was the trade name of the first wholly man-made plastic, a process of moulding discovered by Leo Baekaland in 1907, a name that has become synonymous with nostalgia and collecting.

This huge collection of design and social history conjures reminiscence through shape, colour and use. Early wooden-cased refrigerators — including the Beehive, with its cooling mechanism on top — are among the large domestic appliances on the ground floor. The ovens were part of that labour-saving dream sold to housewives in the 1930s. Both the Parkinson Cowan — in cream with cherry-red trim — and the New World models, evoke the streamlined designs of Norman Bel Geddes and Raymond Loewy. My 'London' gas oven, given by a friend, has the same red dials and modernist lettering, and cooks well without any fancy thermostat!

Such pieces show how the plastic moulding process enabled industrial designers to challenge accepted forms. The telephone was made of plastic; as well as the familiar black models there is a green version for War Office use in 1940. Electric heaters took on new shapes — round and squat in the 1945 model by HMV. What was once sold in Woolworth's and considered kitsch, is now fashionably collectable: napkin rings; pink biscuit barrels with transfer patterns of crinoline ladies; and bright cruet sets. And we are entertained in the period by the gentle strains of Ray Noble and his orchestra, which follow us up the stairs to the first floor, where there are some early, lethal-looking hairdryers and a dentist's chair. After climbing further to see the milling equipment on the top floor, tea calls.

Both lunch and tea are served in the Georgian house nearby, or in the garden; the tearoom has some of the owner's collection and carefully chosen furnishings. There is a Keith Murray pot and a painting of the mill by Liz Lawrence, while a blue period bar fire warms the visitors. Surprisingly this is one of the few museum cafés in the county, and one of the best, and there is the unusual bonus of bed and breakfast beside a museum.

Tea comes in blue Denby cups with fruitcake or scones baked with a light touch, with generous servings of clotted cream, and strawberry or whortleberry jam. Whortleberries were once sold by the whortleberry higgler, who travelled around the Brendons and Exmoor crying 'Wurts, Wurts', with his 'dusky purple fruit, newly gathered and savouring of earth and dew', piled on his cart, as described by Berta Lawrence.

But at the end of the lane, the Williton church has a disturbing association, with Sir Reginald Fitzurse who was born here and was one of the four who killed Sir Thomas à Becket at Canterbury. It is set among cottages, orchards, a green and a cross. Penance of another kind, not always earned, were part of the tasks inmates had to carry out in the Williton workhouse in Long Street. This was designed by Sir George Gilbert Scott and William Moffat around 1835 and has been sensitively converted; it was one of fifty built by the practice but the only listed Grade II*example in Somerset – a fine looking building designed on the cruciform plan.

My own bonus for these western trips is staying at a beautiful farmhouse where I am always welcomed by the family and their animals. One small Jack Russell, Binker, has a character three times his size. And in spite of his penchant for my boots and sheep skin gloves, I cannot but admire his good taste. We have become true friends. In the summer I can walk down to the sea with the dogs, or wake to the sight of the beasts grazing and see nesting house martins at close quarters. This is as much a privilege as the smell of the hay in the barns in the winter, or seeing the first daffodils in the lane. I know my breakfast egg has been carried a few yards, the tomatoes a few feet. I leave reluctantly but always completely refreshed.

Watchet: creative currents at the seaside town

Watchet, once an important harbour town, has an air of fifty-year-old summers. Do not be deceived by appearances. Lift the odd curtain, open a door and you find a strong current of contemporary art and culture flowing through the town.

Proud of its historical pedigree, it is mentioned in the 'Exon' or Exeter Domesday Survey. Earlier, the Danes made their first landing here in 918. It was one of the twelve manors in Somerset directly owned by Edward the Confessor and there are strong Norman connections. Even earlier Watchet was a port, and had a Saxon mint — denoting the settlement's importance. In fact, Watchet coins are displayed in the Copenhagen, Stockholm and British Museums — evidence of Danegeld, the tax imposed on the local population by the Danish invaders, the proceeds of which were later buried by the Anglo-Saxons.

Although Watchet was never agriculturally rich, the sea and the land have been its key to survival and its proximity to Bristol and Wales have brought wealth. Watchet's sea trade has gone but it is not downhearted. How many other towns with a population of 1,200, have two museums — a series of winter lectures organised by one — amateur dramatics, artists, musicians, a carnival, a superb art gallery and importantly a harbour-side railway station? And there is another association, as Coleridge may well have started his epic poem *The Rime of the Ancient Mariner* at the Bell, after he and Wordsworth walked here through 'sheltered valleys close by the seaside'. As Coleridge walked with Hazlitt on another journey he pointed out the 'red-orbed disk of the setting sun on the horizon', like the ship in that poem.

Making the most of its assets, this 'funny little town' inspires visitors and artists who have lived here, in many cases all their lives, and more who have become hooked. It is the same old story: buildings make a great contribution to atmosphere, but the people who inhabit them imbue a place with a living character.

Watchet folk revere the past but without affectation. Grand architecture no, but a splendid perpendicular church, a sprinkling of good Georgian and vernacular cottages, the sea, hills and the most sought-after fossil hunting ground in the county.

Stone is Watchet's bedrock. And fortunately Dr Eric Robinson, an eminent geologist, is on hand, having retired here, and he rejoices in sharing his knowledge: 'geology is in the blood and experience of Watchet'. His passion and experience comes through in a series of leaflets that make the geology accessible and enlightens all fossil hunters. The stone is varied, traded and travelled. Firstly limestone, which when burnt with clay produces cement. Watchet has blue Lias from the Jurassic period, found on the coast at East Quay beach; gypsum was collected from the red rock cliffs then shipped to Bristol where it was used to make plaster of Paris. Alabaster was also exported.

Slate was another important building material that was mined locally at Treborough, and exported; red sandstone was quarried near Williton; whilst iron ore, mined in the Brendons, was brought in on the dedicated Mineral Line directly to the harbour. Moreover stone was brought from other counties, as ballast on the return trips from Wales and Plymouth. White limestone makes a sharp contrast in West Street with, for example, the sandstone at the library, once the former lifeboat house, which also has yellow clay bricks made at Ebbw Vale.

As the sea trade declined and port incomes fell in the eighteenth century, so the town had to embrace change and land-based industries began in earnest around 1750, with papermaking; the Wansborough Mill is a descendent of the original mill, now employing 200 people. Flourmills have continued a 1,000-year tradition and were productive in the early twentieth century, exporting to Ireland and Scandinavia. But the harbour eventually closed down in the 1980s and is now being used as a marina, for pleasure.

Watchet welcomed the railway in 1868, which cut its iron path through fields owned by the Luttrells, and so the focus changed and tourists arrived. The little station, which was once the end of the line, buzzes with eager travellers, and the volunteers who tend the platform, as throughout all the West Somerset Railway, take a pride in it. Watchet also has its own mosaic artwork, showing the local variety of stone: the Jubilee Wall was made, under the guidance of Eric Robinson, by a group of young people with special needs whose work must be admired by many thousands of visitors.

Through the spring, summer and autumn the sound and sight of the trains raises the spirits of all those who see the engine pulling in from Williton and Will's Neck beyond, being the high point of the Quantock Hills. With the steam billowing behind, this is a Mcknight Kauffer poster come alive. On its last lap to Minehead the train travels inland, following the Washford River and the Doniford Brook, then back again to the sea at Blue Anchor and so on to Dunster and Minehead.

Watchet has a small eclectic mix of shops where you find the summer deck shoes only found by the sea. There is a chemist, a baker, an ironmonger, several antique and bric-a-brac emporia and the exceptional gallery. Recently, a small delicatessen has arrived and is supporting the local producers.

But the parish church of St Decuman is separate from the town on a hill. It was founded by a Celtic missionary in the sixth century, who sailed from Wales in a leather boat called a curragh, long before the Saxons arrived. And an ancient well, possibly dating from AD 400, has brought pilgrims for its healing powers, and further explains the church's position. It was built in 1100, on land owned by the first Luttrell of East Quantoxhead, but as Watchet was part of the parish of Williton it owes much to the patronage of the Wyndham family, descended by marriage from the Fitzurse family. They continued to pay for prayers to be said at the church of the Holy Cross, now above the Market House museum, for the soul of their ill-famed ancestor, Reginald.

All the patronage is reflected in the style, decoration and fabric of the pleasing church with yet another wagon roof and rood screen. The oldest window is in the south aisle, which, with the chancel, is rendered cream, shining with the morning sun. Both the tower and north aisle are faced with red ashlar and the mullions are Dundry stone brought down from Bristol, by sea. The chancel is thirteenth century and the fine tower is a scaled down replica of St Michael's at Minehead with carvings let into the niches on each quarter; one has a carving of its patron saint. Here I noticed the up-ended stone roof slates with a hatched pattern set into the floor of the porch — giving the entrance an interesting chequerboard pattern and later again in Minehead at St Michael's. Texture, pattern and colour are found in the beautiful twelfth-century encaustic tiles in the choir. These tiles, in muted medieval colours, were rescued from nearby Cleeve Abbey. Watchet's most colourful memorials are to John Wyndham and his wife, who are kneeling, showing, through the carving, the folds of the dress and rich style of Jacobean fashion. Both the church and the town have enough colour to make up for the sometimes grey sea.

Through the centuries Watchet connections can be made with court and literature. In Geoffrey Chaucer's *The Miller's Tale* we find a 'Kirtel of light Watchett', a pale hyacinth blue. This sky-coloured cloth was also worn by sixteenth-century mariners. Like other west country towns, Watchet continues to celebrate one of its ancient customs with their Court Leet held every year in October. Until the nineteenth century this ceremony – where town officers had to swear their allegiance to the court – included the scavenger, constable and ale taster. The last is the only post that is perpetuated and the ceremony concludes, of course, with dinner and punch; the recipe, according to Ben Norman, who has written about Watchet and its nautical past, is a secret!

How appropriate that the quay has acquired a large sculpture to celebrate the millennium representing the Ancient Mariner with his 'long grey beard and glittering eye'; powerful and holding the fallen albatross and crossbow — 'alone, alone, all, all alone'.

One is far from alone with the jumble of fish and chip shops, cafés and pubs, so peculiar to the English seaside, across the way. And where would we be without them? The Market House Museum near the harbour attracts at least 36,000 visitors a year! Its mix of social history and geology works well and all the artefacts are displayed in easy-to-see cabinets. The sea flows through every century of history. Here you might have your first encounter with the history of the great storm of 1901, which almost destroyed the harbour; the Wyndham estate gave 200 elms to repair the damage and the disaster brought the townsfolk together to raise funds and rebuild their livelihood.

In another case the mariner's tools are displayed with evil-looking bodkins, among those kept in his canvas 'diddy bag'. Reminding us that the entire coast was vulnerable, there is a picture of the Armada defence system put up along the north Somerset coast, and there are tales of Watchet shipwrights. Emerging nineteenth-century social developments are chronicled in a photograph by Watchet's first photographer, James Date. One of his glass plates shows the butcher and the landlord of the London Inn, about to purchase a side of mutton in front of a black background, adding a sense of occasion.

By the railway station, the Boat Museum is solely dedicated to the flattie or flatner — a flat-bottomed boat only used and found in the estuary of the River Parrett: for fishing around Bridgwater and at Watchet. It was designed to cope with shallow water only and was probably copied from Viking boats, constructed from one piece of wood. These useful vessels carried withies and peat around the rhynes and may well have been used in the flood years.

In Swain Street there is even more colour and surprise at the Lynda Cotton gallery — *a tour de force* of art and antique furniture. Such quality is surprising in a small town, let alone a small gallery. Nick and Lynda Cotton also provide a platform for new work during Somerset Art Weeks. But throughout the year they assiduously champion local artists, alongside beautiful late nineteenth- and early twentieth-century work in the landscape genre of the artists of the Newlyn School. Moreover their generosity and knowledge, sharing everything of art and Somerset with me during these last few years, has been invaluable.

The Market House Museum shows its wares.

Two years ago I saw the work of Watchet painter Jenny Baron, and last year seeing Jennifer Dagworthy's work led me to meet her in Minehead. By the sea, with unbelievable views, Jennifer sees depth in the coast and landscape, by day and night. I like her after-dark images, which remind us how much there is to see with, and the vulnerability of, natural light. Her concern with texture is apparent not just in her materials — she uses beautiful hand-made paper from Two Rivers Mill at Roadwater and coloured inks — but she has the ability to picture, for example, the stone in her harbour wall images, that we are drawn to touch.

Sue Onley, whose exciting work is on this cover, had her first show here last year. She explores and paints the fields, coast and hedges of west Somerset with the eye of an archaeological draughtsman; her parents' cartographical skills also seem to have been inherited. Sue is mapping the landscape, emboldening the features with a brave palette. There are the familiar names of Ian Cryer — who paints intimate scenes of everyday life — and the work of John Walker, whose boat and fishing ensembles owe much to the St Ives School. Jenny Baron opens her studio at the top of Causeway Terrace, with stunning views of Bridgwater Bay, beyond her vegetable garden. She paints still life — fruit, vegetables and fossils using watercolour, achieving fascinating results with her own invented process. Shallots, quinces and borlotti beans become desirable objects against a black background. The style may recall old masters, but the work is utterly contemporary in execution.

You can make your own search for fossils similar to those that have inspired Jenny if you spend time on Doniford Beach, looking towards Kilve. Here I saw children collecting some tremendous examples. And hearing a little lad exclaiming his luck at finding a devil's toenail taught me something completely new!

Dunster: the castle and village

Can there be anything left to write about a place where all the superlatives have been spent? Undeniably, Dunster is unsurpassed. Its ancient buildings — a castle in an exquisite setting on one hill and a picturesque tower on the other — make it one of the most often-used images for illustrating England. But each season brings a difference. Arrive, as I have, on a sunny morning in September and the whole scene is one of expectation. See it in winter in a snow flurry and it is another place, all the more visible without the clutter of cars. Or arrive in the summer at the station at Dunster beach from Watchet and see another aspect and the highly desirable beach huts.

But in Dunster one begins at the much-photographed, gabled, octagonal Yarn Market of 1589. This open market, both elegant and functional, was designed to sell cloth and has it all: wide eaves, timber beams, dormer windows and a small crowning lantern. Close by, facing the Market Place, the Luttrell Arms, once the residence of the abbots of Cleeve Abbey, has welcomed travellers for 500 years. And it earns its architectural place in Sir Albert Richardson's 1923 *Inns of England*. Following the Reformation in the 1600s it was altered by George Luttrell and has an overmantel which Nikolaus Pevsner considered was of the same hand as one dated 1620, in the castle. Within is an interesting courtyard gallery with fine carving, contrasting with the stone front, now creeper-covered; and look for the secret garden

The Jettied Nunnery

179

at first-floor level, at the end of the gallery, offering another glorious aspect towards the castle.

From here the High Street dives down through the village turning in front of the first castle gate to continue past the unusual, jettied, Nunnery – a fourteenth-century house in narrow Church Street which has three storeys. Then the road reaches Dunster Mill, the Pack Horse Bridge, whitewashed cottages and on to Exmoor.

The castle story begins with the De Mohun family, who arrived with William the Conqueror. They built this fortress, seen from and looking out over miles of the surrounding countryside. It is difficult to imagine that the sea once washed the site; now there are fertile plantations of trees including a 100-year-old lemon tree that flourishes in the gardens. The acclaimed essayist Hazlitt, walking with Coleridge and John Chester of Nether Stowey, on their way to the Valley of the Rocks, saw Dunster as a landscape painting, 'a small town between the brow of the hill and the sea, I remember it wistfully as it lay below; contrasted with the woody scene around, it looked as clear, as pure, as *embrowned* (his italics) as any landscape I have seen since of Gaspar Poussin or of Domenichino'.

So they did not see the cottages either side of the main thoroughfare, with apparently Georgian elevations, running between the hilly terminals, which once looked out over large cattle markets. Neither would they have seen the bay windows and cobbled pathways, which today sport blue and green in window frames and porches, which alone are worth a vernacular journey. No house is finer than its neighbour but the whole length of this spontaneous development is a model of its type.

At the castle, the thirteenth-century gateway is the oldest remaining part of the Norman original, reached after a steep climb from the village. This approach passes a most unusual seventeenth-century stable block, which in the early twentieth century housed the horses that were ridden in the polo tournaments held on Dunster lawn. It is now the shop for this National Trust-owned property. With original 'boxes' the fittings demonstrate the importance and value given to horses. You arrive at what is principally a Jacobean mansion; remodelled between 1868 and 1872 by Anthony Salvin. He was a prolific castle architect: of Alnwick, Petworth for the Egremonts in Sussex, and Warwick.

This period of remodelling triggers a literary connection with a novel by Thomas Hardy set, quite unusually, in Somerset. It is worth speculating about his use of Dunster Castle and this part of west Somerset as a means of expressing intrigue, romance always, and architectural practice. He wrote *A Laodicean* during a long period of illness and enforced rest. In his preface Hardy hints at the architectural developments behind the novel. His polemic being that times were changing in country manors and mansions, and that what occurs in the book had been supported by evidence of incidents that were taking place in most counties. Thus the castle in the story becomes the subject of debate over the style changes that his client, Paula Power its owner, wishes to make to her newly inherited property.

The geographical facts may not have the same exactitude as his other Wessex novels, which Hermann Lea in his analysis so cleverly decodes. In our case Toneborough, being Taunton, is too near; nevertheless the architect hero is called George Somerset, Stancy Castle could be Dunster, a railway station is featured and Markton as Dunster village is perfectly credible; even the Luttrell Arms appears as The Lord Quantock Arms — wrong hills but the picture comes to life. In this novel of 'ingenuity', Hardy takes every opportunity to inform his readers of his knowledge of architectural history and practice.

Somerset is invited to make drawings to alter the castle, for a competition (involving trickery on his opponent's part) to be judged by the RIBA, while winning the heroine's hand involves another kind of competition. During their meetings Somerset and Paula converse and parry as Hardy brings

The courtyard at the Luttrell Arms

in the nineteenth-century Battle of the Styles, eclecticism and the accurate drawing of the original medieval. Somerset first meets her when he is sketching Markton church. Written in 1881, eight years after Salvin's new work, was Hardy, as he says in his preface, parodying the vogue for alterations in general?

In fact Dunster is completely synonymous with the Luttrell family, who held the castle for 600 years until 1976; to this family we owe the best of the interior architecture because they commissioned the finest artists and craftsmen, especially during the Restoration. From this period the carved oak staircase, with its pierced balustrade of elm, measuring nine inches thick, makes the climb a rare experience. One has to examine this narrative in wood, which celebrates the re-flowering of art and architecture and the Luttrells' lives. From the newel post, festooned with fruit, putti, ebullient sunflowers, coins, hunting scenes, acanthus leaves and classical egg and dart pattern, this is a beautiful allegorical work.

Similar themes reappear in 'one of the most gorgeous plaster ceilings in England' and the small withdrawing room of 1681. Two hundred years later we can see Salvin's muscular castle style permeating the entrance to the muniment room and a door, studded for strength. Although he did re-use the fifteenth-century fireplace to provide seats for the spectators in the room which personifies grand Victorian living and the separation of the sexes — the billiard room.

More utilitarian it may be, but the bathroom is quite a star. It is built in mahogany and is supposedly the oldest in Somerset. On the room name boards, hanging in the servants' bell room, there are further reminders of the household, its organisation and size. And a 1930s bedroom fireplace is left just as it was found.

In Hardy's novel, plays were performed at Stancy Castle, whereas many of today's events and drama for visitors are staged on the Green Court. Below in the fifteen-acre parkland and in gardens there is more pleasure throughout the whole year due to their position: they are sheltered and face south. Plants therefore grow abundantly, with species flowering earlier than in other parts of the county. I have seen vinca and primroses in January. The magnolia can bloom in early March, and usually by Easter visitors will be able to smell the scent of mimosa. To the west are those bracken-covered slopes that Hazlitt saw, close enough for the hunting lords to pinpoint their quarry before the chase.

Even so, this isn't the only surprising garden. Near the parish church, the walled Dunster village garden is carefully tended with cordons of cultivated mulberry trees and perennials. From this garden you can see the rising hill of Conygar and its folly — a beacon for miles. The walled memorial garden also has two long borders. Behind there is a dovecote twenty feet high with four feet wide walls; possibly one of the most ancient examples in the country and with a revolving ladder. The eggs were collected by means of this ladder, fixed to the arm of a vertical post made of ash. This 400-year-old device or 'Potence', which replaced a Norman original, proves that good design and engineering survive!

If you want see more carvings, St George's church has some of the best in one of the widest rood screens in the country; built to settle a dispute over church organisation between the monks of the Benedictine order and the parishioners, led by their priest. To enable both sides to retain their space and rights in what was once one large nave, the matter was settled at Glastonbury in 1498. This screen is surmounted by a loft or gallery and features fifty compartments; only oak develops this patina with age. One of the oldest memorials is to Adam of Cheddar, who was Prior of Dunster between 1335 and 1355. Nearby are the former monks' lodgings and the great medieval tithe barn, which, with the dovecote, formed the monastic range.

During one long August day, the Dunster Show affords another kind of spectacle. This is staged triumphantly on the field in front of the castle. When I visited, there was an archery competition on one side of the hill, in the foreground rows of tethered beasts and pens of sheep, cosseted and brushed by their white-coated owners. Beyond I heard the sounds of jousting as it may have been, but now with a loudspeaker as well as the cheering crowds. Each breed looked their best: the Devon Red Rubies, the curly-coated Herefords; the exquisite cream brushed coats of the Exmoor Horn sheep, the solid Black Angus cattle, the golden prize-winning Jersey with penetrating velvety brown eyes which belonged to a family farm, just the other side of the road. Last year, they creatively planted their field margins with sunflowers and brightened the road to Minehead.

Accepting that in Dunster village shopping is more geared to tourists, the 1,200 residents can still buy items of use at the hardware shop and papers from the newsagent, send letters from the post office and buy groceries, and very good cheese, from the delicatessen. And in the last two years, with the opening of a new bookshop and an antiquarian book dealer, there is the encouraging proof that culture is on the ascendancy; adding to the already established charming studio of potters, John and Jano Clarke, and the well-known gallery run by the Somerset Guild of Craftsmen.

A handful of these west Somerset villages and pubs have acquired exciting contemporary sculpture and signs. And as Dunster is a perfect centre for walking, seeing the work of Rachel Reckitt in Rodhuish, or even Roadwater, is a rewarding excercise. At Roadwater her sign for the Valiant Soldier Inn is a triumph; almost Hardyean, in blue coat, thigh-high boots and with the sort of moustache that Captain de Stancy might have sported in *A Laodicean*.

Also in Roadwater her father, Norman, designed the Arts and Crafts village hall, opened in 1928. This created a performance space for drama; where meetings and dinners are held; and where supporters may watch cricket from a pleasant barn-inspired building. Miss Reckitt lived for many years at Golsancott. At Rodhuish, in the white, unlit church of St Bartholomew I saw her metal sculpture of Jacob and the Angel — an extraordinary experience. As Jacob struggles with the Angel, he kneels with its wings soaring above like propeller blades. The successful combination of this rural church and contemporary work defies most preconceptions of how art might be placed in such a small church.

Chapter 8

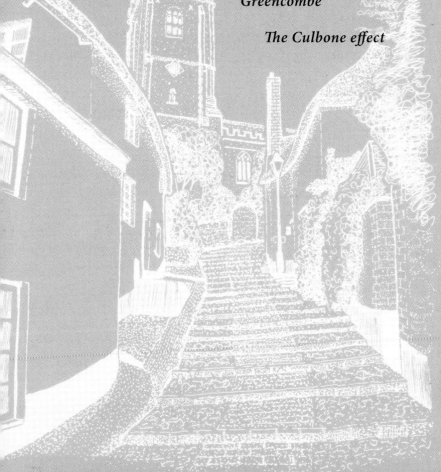

Minehead and more beside the sea

A harmonious quartet: Selworthy, Allerford, Bossington and Luccombe

Porlock: the museum and Greencombe

The Culbone effect

Minehead and more beside the sea

A stunning location, a mild climate, hills, coast, a surprising variety of architecture and history? Not many would associate all this with Minehead — rather thinking resort and honey pots. But just over 100 years ago people from all parts of the country and the continent came and built grand houses to take advantage of Minehead's attributes, including a wealthy Scottish confectioner and a retired tea planter. Those who didn't build rented, bringing their families and staff for the summer months. Hotels sprang up, a theatre was opened, tearooms did good business – and all to provide diversion and entertainment for the sophisticated visitor.

If you arrive at the terminus of the West Somerset Railway, you can see — as many of those tourists also did — the whitewashed cottages and appealing green slopes of North Hill and the tower of St Michael's church. Like many I had stayed here as a child and it is those memories that usually encourage people to return and retire here. As it did 100 years ago, so today the mix and energy of new arrivals sparks new interests and culture.

I became fascinated with Minehead's growth from a small fishing village with the safest harbour in Somerset, even well-built in the 1720s when Daniel Defoe found it full of rich merchants. For 300 years until 1800 herrings and wool were traded with Ireland, Virginia and the West Indies. Interestingly, the pier was constructed in 1610 and enlarged in 1901, which coincided with more visitors and the paddle steamer trips that continue to steam along the coast to Ilfracombe and Lundy.

Although the herring shoals had left for other waters by the end of the eighteenth century, another industry was not far behind — tourism, and the search for the picturesque. One could call William Gilpin one of the prime proponents and his description of the sea around Minehead as being 'beautifully variegated and formed of kindred colours' would have encouraged artists and his followers.

In 1800, before the railway reached Minehead, Reverend Richard Warner arrived from Bath where by now folk were swimming in 'commodious bathing machines' — as they did at Brightlingsea, now Brighton. The lodgings were reasonable, the provisions plentiful and the air 'soft and salubrious'. He stayed at

The Harbour and North Hill, Minehead

the Plume of Feathers, his 'delightful caravanserai' which stood at a point between Wellington Square, the Avenue and opposite Friday Street. Although Warner's genteel Minehead had access to 'decent turnpike roads', its distance from London was sufficient to deter what he called 'felicity hunters'.

In J.M.W. Turner's topographical engraving of 1830, Minehead and the harbour were undeveloped. But forty years later another engraving shows more houses on North Hill. One hundred years after Warner's 'tour', a letter in the *West Somerset Free Press* praised the resort and its first-class postal arrangements, as letters arrived in Bristol on the very day they were posted.

Until 1874 Minehead consisted of the higher town; the church and its surrounding cottages; the harbour with fishermen's cottages and their protective doors. This is principally what Defoe saw as well as a handful of medieval buildings including The Priory with wooden mullions, now seen in the Avenue.

For me the following decades of the town's development are exciting, as some of England's, and in one case, Scotland's, leading architects, made their mark in here. As the burgeoning manufacturing classes had the wherewithal to redefine their interiors and, in some cases build anew, so architects could provide them with houses fitting their new position.

One of the first was Clevelands, built above the church and designed by Foster and Wood of Bristol in 1877. Clevelands has a large amount of black and white timber decoration on its essentially brick, asymmetrical front. With five gables, the large first-floor balconies must give amazing views. The census revealed that in 1910, the Baroness le Clement de Taintegnies lived here; a name that adds a Parisian dimension to Minehead — of the *belle époque*.

By 1903 engravings of North Hill show that Elgin Tower had been built. This is a large embattled house with a tower, designed by brothers William and Alexander Reid of Elgin for Mr McKenzie, a Scottish confectioner, in 1886. The castellated mansion was faced with sandstone transported from Elgin in north-east Scotland. Its parapets, cannon and unrivalled position must have caused much head turning when it was complete. Whilst this grand statement continues in the entrance hall, designed for receiving and entertaining, the reception rooms have an unexpected cool, neo-classical character. The windows are magnificent. Apart from the drawing room with its showpiece plaster fireplace, detailing is restrained, mostly derived from the skilfully conceived profiles of the dado rail, articulated arches and generous skirting board. This is a rare Somerset example of the classical and civic work for which the architects are famed in Elgin. And it reflects what the

Reids had learnt from their uncle, also a 'classical' man.

Elgin Tower makes the very best of the extraordinary light, the sea and the hills. For the last four years the artist Jennifer Dagworthy and her husband have lived here, restoring it with love and taking inspiration from the changing sea, landscape and seasons. During Somerset Art Weeks we are fortunate to have the opportunity to see her work.

Northfield is another large house built in 1903, for Mr R.B. Major, a wealthy tea planter. It was sold in 1946, since when it has been a hotel. The sale catalogue listed seventeen bedrooms, stables and a butler's pantry. One can see the double drawing room with harbour views; an oak-panelled library; and elegant staircase – the latter mostly original when I last visited. Because riding and polo were very much part of Minehead's Edwardian society, Major was able to offer hospitality to Indian maharajahs who came to play polo on the lawns of Dunster. Despite the sale of both stables and walled kitchen garden, in the design of the sizeable garden we can see the influence of Gertrude Jekyll's prevailing style; Northfield has stone paths, a long arbour and stone columns with planting patterns emulating her signature, and she did, after all, work at Hestercombe with Sir Edwin Lutyens.

Kildare Lodge was also built in 1903 in Townsend Road, but there the similarity ends, except that its architect Barry Parker — an Arts and Crafts practitioner — had been a pupil of Lutyens. He is best known for his partnership with Raymond Unwin and their joint housing project at Letchworth Garden Suburb. The client was Dr Newman, but his connection with Parker and Minehead is not yet apparent. This house was also surrounded by a large garden. It has the medievalising elements that William Morris and his contemporaries employed in their houses. Here, surprisingly, there is original door furniture and copper decoration above some of the fireplaces. And one can see the influence in the windows and semicircular steps that Lutyens had used for Deanery Gardens, in Berkshire.

Parker and Unwin, like Voysey, considered comfort and function as important as the artistic elements and craftsmanship. There are some good examples in the Parks of the lessons learnt from this design vocabulary where functional features — chimney breasts, eaves and entrances — are expressed, and the essence of cottage vernacular, fitting this region, is often emphasised.

To see St Michaels church and the older cottages of the Higher Town involves a steady climb from Wellington Square, passing the Almshouses given by Robert Quirke in 1620 and just restored. His life and work is celebrated both here and at St Peter-on-the-Quay — a tiny church dedicated to sailors, with a contemporary stained-glass window by Clare Maryann Green of Porlock.

From the quay or North Road and for views, the cobbled Church Path is unparalleled where the growth of the cottages – two called Cider Apple and Pink — appears random, yet each fits, garden and all, like a jigsaw. St John's however, which may have been a lockup, with wooden mullions and leaded lights, stands out in sandstone.

The church of St Michael is a surprisingly large, parish church with Norman origins and a fourteenth-century bell tower. The carvings on the rood screen, the pulpit and the communion table are superb and, dating from the fifteenth century justify the measured drawing published by the Architectural Association in 1882. This screen emulates that at Dunster, with fine tracery and springing from the piers between the bays. The font is perpendicular and the pulpit Jacobean. And Minehead has a version of the famous clock at Wells, but their Jack Hammer — a green hooded Manikin — is now quiet.

I came out of the church to meet the facing cottage within touching distance and spoke to the owner who was born and had lived here for eighty-one years. Having been christened and married at St Michael's, she would not wish to be anywhere else. Surrounded by exquisite views, other gardens full of beans, sun-loving agapanthus and a walnut tree, I had to agree.

Continuity is a precious commodity, and in a different strand Minehead must have celebrated its ancient May Day custom, the dance of the Sailors' Hobby Horse — for centuries. As the horse dances around the town accompanied by drum and accordion, children follow. It is made of hazel and willow in the shape of an upturned coracle, covered with hessian and decorated with brightly-coloured rag strips. Some say it is taken around to ward off danger and to protect sailors; folklore seems to prefer an ancient fertility rite; another plausible origin is that it was made to scare off the Danish invaders.

St Peter on the Quay

On the esplanade along which the horse dances there is an unusual sculpture by Sarah Ward, made in metal and with the intention of encouraging walkers rather than warding off strangers. Not easy to miss; the large pair of hands hold a map, marking the beginning of the South West Coastal Path. Everyone I met or know in Minehead walks; south to Grabbist Hill, or to Dunster, to Selworthy and Exmoor.

Not so far to the gates of Blenheim Gardens, given to the town by Mr Major in 1902, where folk dancing and concerts did and still take place. Minehead's parks and planting have a prize-winning reputation; indeed it has the feel of a garden town. And travelling on the bus to Porlock I could appreciate the series of interconnecting green spaces, bridges and walks that have become the Parks, a short distance from Wellington Square.

By the 1920s the famous Blue Motor Coach Company had arrived and superseded the horse-drawn coaches that started here, taking passengers to and from Lynton, with a great deal of opposition. However the poet Rosemary Burnett, who lives in Minehead, recalls some coach and four trips to Dulverton driven by a Captain Hewitt, which started at the Plume of Feathers, as late as 1960. Many residents regret the loss of the Inn and its replacement.

As you write your postcard among the birch trees planted to green up Wellington Square, which form a small piazza, you sit near a rare and uncommonly fine statue of Queen Anne, made by Francis Bird in 1719 and moved here in the late 1880s. Although trees mask the north façade of St Andrew's, towerless and the last of G.E. Street's many high Victorian churches, completed in 1880, the unadorned interior needs to be seen. Complementing this character some good, contemporary oak doors with new door furniture and an oak altar rail have been recently designed in conjunction with Caroe and Partners of Wells.

Minehead still has several independent food shops around the corner and in the Avenue an excellent health shop, tearooms and a Farmers' Market. Warner would have enjoyed the service you receive at Gerald David the butcher, where the localness of joints and sides, Exmoor lamb and free-range chicken, is proclaimed with a sign stating 'English' in the window.

There are film, history and civic societies and a theatre in a former art deco cinema. Off the wide tree-lined Avenue, opposite the town hall by W.J. Tamlyn, Banckes Street flaunts Minehead's turn of the nineteenth-century civic face. There are swags and roses on the Exmoor Masonic Hall, of 1889; a classical style for the Church Institute, whilst the building originally for the Brethren in 1903, has since 1976 been the Friends Meeting House. Among the plethora of groups who use this, I found another Friday Country Market, where beautiful flowers, raspberry jam and local honey were sold. But with a four-hour walk ahead, discovering Minehead I could not alas, overload the rucksack!

A harmonious quartet: Selworthy, Allerford, Bossington and Luccombe

Selworthy, Allerford, Bossington, and Luccombe are four among several beautiful villages on the 2,500-acre Holnicote Estate that was given by Richard Acland to the National Trust in 1944.

From John Gaze's history of the National Trust we learn that Hardwick Rawnsley, a member of the founding four, rode over the estate on horseback in 1921. Hardly surprising that the picturesque Selworthy cottages won him over: 'saw many houses that day upon the Holnicote estate and not one of them ... but made us feel an artist had planned it and would wish to have a chance of drawing it'. He rode on over the Packhorse Bridge at Allerford, undeniably one of the most photographed settings in England, over rich arable land. They must have ridden through these incomparable villages that are now protected, with their lime-washed, often cob, walls, their thatch, their rotund, laterally-positioned bread ovens and the gardens. And they went on as we can still walk, through the Allerford plantation from Selworthy, filled with silver fir, spruce, Douglas pine, chestnut, Wellingtonia and walnut.

Selworthy makes an auspicious beginning. The first of the four, although hidden from the main road, is on the journey from Minehead to Porlock. It is cradled by its namesake beacon, at the top of an avenue overarched with ash and oak. A mile or so and the first sight of the golden walls comes into view, hinting at what lies ahead: two or three houses and a farm and then the famous seven thatched cottages clustered around Selworthy Green. Although detached they are integral to one another. Their Gothick design and grouping may have been influenced by what Acland had seen of John Nash's work at Blaise Hamlet near Bristol — Romantic Gothick in the extreme. Two of the originals at Selworthy have been pulled down and before 1828, when Sir Thomas Acland remodelled them for estate pensioners as almshouses, one might imagine them as more humble cottages. The green would have been less manicured with more common grazing and all that implies; with beasts tethered and a tithe barn.

In 1831 there were thirty-one houses in the parish with 483 inhabitants, which explains the size of the church at the top of the village; this, with its original porch door and linenfold panels, opens onto Exmoor. It is the pinnacle of the village and has just been re-lime-washed in bright white, a lavish church for its hidden-awayness. Looking south to Dunkery Beacon, the large perpendicular windows and fine tracery in the south aisle catch the full sun.

An unmistakable west Somerset cottage chimney at Bossington tea gardens

The interior is an exercise in contrasting styles of carving and decoration. An original wagon roof in the south aisle, although repaired, is, as Pevsner writes, 'one of the finest in the county'. The wall plates are embellished with angels and the bosses with symbols of the Passion. The delightfully classical west gallery added in 1750 is set within carved Doric pilasters and an oak frieze. Above the porch the Aclands built their own 'delicious little Gothic pavilion' the equivalent to the box or squire's pew. Having slender carving, it is more akin to a private opera box than a pew. However the central core of the church is much older, with a simple Norman font — but the majority is of the fourteenth century, on an older Saxon site.

Some years ago my daughter and I were staying near Wiveliscombe; we saw Dunster, went to Watersmeet and came here: such a lovely moment — enjoying our tea with scones, cream and jam, of course, after walking above on the Beacon — that I felt it needed photographing. Afterwards when I was lecturing to clients or students I would put up the slide I took that afternoon — the view from Periwinkle Cottage's tea garden — as an example of what visitors from far and wide yearn for in Somerset, in England. The peace, good simple food and views remain. Only the resolute slimmer could resist the ritual of a Selworthy cream tea, or one from the spread of homemade cakes laid out inside Periwinkle Cottage, on the buffet. This tearoom has one of the best locations in the county and I recently found a naïve little watercolour depicting the same scene at a local show. I had it framed and hung it above my desk, where it is a constant reminder of this location.

The Packhorse Bridge at Allerford

Near Selworthy Green on the east side of the lane, a small plaque on the side of another tithe barn marks where the famous puppeteer, Walter Wilkinson, and his wife spent the last years of their extraordinary lives. Each day Walter, who founded and wrote *The Peep Show* in 1926, walked through the Selworthy woods until his late 80s. With his own contribution to culture he toured Somerset, the west country and later America. He made his puppets and proscenium arch, which he wheeled around on a homemade contraption he named The Encumbrance. To begin with he only had one fellow to assist him, but later his wife also helped. Those who reviewed his books included J.B. Priestley and Arnold Bennett, and his American experiences have recently been serialised in a BBC Radio 4 reading. Winifred Wilkinson was also equally productive in her later years, publishing three books from Selworthy. One attracted much critical acclaim, being the combination of what she saw in Europe after both world wars, worlds away from the peace of Selworthy.

It is only a short and undemanding hike across the road to the Holnicote Estate headquarters where another writer lived in elegant converted kennels – the composer and writer Vivian Ellis. Such productions as *Bless the Bride*, and such catchy melodies as 'Bella Marguerita' were his, and of course the 'Coronation Scot', the theme tune used for the famous Paul Temple series, which brings back everything Home Service. Mr Morcomb, who lives in Selworthy told me, this was composed by Ellis on the railway line from London to Taunton!

Next Allerford — perhaps half an hour through the woods, or minutes on wheels — to the packhorse bridge to which Pevsner accords one simple line: 'two arches; very picturesque'. But expect more: a museum, a post office with a tea garden, more cottages and a woodland walk to Lynch, Bossington and the coast. In any event a bus timetable gives you the freedom to hail one at Allerford corner for the next stage or the return journey. The sound of the blacksmith, a sound that Cicily Cooper, the former headmistress, said interrupted the learning, led me to the Allerford museum, once the school where she taught.

Over one summer I walked, looked, had tea in the post office garden and searched out more social history at the museum. Some days were hot, not punishing, but June let itself be known on one walk from Porlock to Allerford where the umbrella in the tea garden was my refuge for writing and shaded the bowl of cream, with more than enough for six. The post office opens for fifteen hours a week, but the shop opens every day, as does the tea garden, all spring and summer long.

One morning I took the 300 bus from Minehead, seeing, as we sailed down the hill, fields covered either by waves of drying hay or newly-shorn sheep, for the museum visit. This is a delightful pick-and-mix sort of place. Of course there is a schoolroom, where the multiplication tables, once embroidered on cloth, hang to remind us of the essential Rs. On other walls there are photographs of Miss Cooper in her hat, looking formal, posing with her mother — with whom she enjoyed picnics at a ripe age — and her certificates for English and Teaching. The schoolroom is neat. The toys are kept carefully; there is a sample of French knitting. Do children do this any more? Pageants and performances are pinned on the wall. But the school, always Church of England, known variously as the Allerford National School, Selworthy Elementary and Voluntary, closed in 1981. So the hall broadens the story with collections and aspects of village life.

Implements used by local industries include a stonebreaker's rake and hammer. Other occupations are remembered with a mole trap and a fish spear. Of the everyday, the cottage hearth — in front of which most family activities took place from washing to drying, and the airing of clothes — has an infant in a rush basket. Shelves support brown teapots, some with decorative bands of pink glaze, that were introduced in the Victorian era. There is a cheese press, a proud portrait of a short horn bull and a photograph of the milk lady from Porlock Dairy. Dennis Corner, the honary curator of Porlock's museum whose family were one of the bakers in Porlock, remembers delivering bread to Miss Cooper during the Second World War.

In her memoirs, Miss Cooper recollects events that affected the village: the arrival of evacuees; the day a stag ran through the village — so exciting that the children left their lessons to see it; the day the Duke of Edinburgh came through Exmoor after the flood disaster of 1952, when the morning started out a 'churlish violet-green, the sullenness of Dunkery sad, and then the sun came out over Hurlestone Point and all was well'. That fateful night of 15 August rain came at 10pm at Allerford and then water poured through her back door.

The walk to Porlock is rich with thatch, heavenly hydrangeas in the front gardens, another tea garden at Bossington or the possibility of a picnic on the beach. In these fields some of the world's best barley is ripened; nourished by the sea breezes and the reflected sun from the hills. I raised this reputation with Mr Morcomb, once the land agent for the estate, who reassured me that an entry had once been sent to the most prestigious grain exhibition in the world, in Canada. Bossington and Porlock won the prize!

Midway, attached to the farmhouse at Lynch, there is a chapel that once belonged to the Sydenhams; for its size, the east window is grand and the tracery emulates the window at Doverhay Manor at Porlock. Miss Cooper remembers a Christmas service here. Even without the tea these villages have their autumn and winter moments when the hills are first cushioned with pink heather, and then later the bracken above Bossington turns and as autumn approaches you see the first puffs of smoke from the large iconic chimneys. For Porlock there is a choice of going either through the fields and by the sea or inland up Bossington Lane, where there is a mixture of twentieth-century houses including the house of Charles E.H. Chadwyck Healey, the historian of these parishes — built in the Arts and Crafts style.

On another afternoon I walked around Luccombe above the church. Looking down I saw the stone and painted cottages, the church and Luccombe (meaning the closed coomb) through the woods. I met riders using this perfect hacking terrain. East Luccombe will be used for the first of an international trekking event in autumn 2006.

Attending special services, in this case Harvest Festival, in country churches gives one a sense of belonging. St Mary's is an

Early English church, with elements of the later perpendicular, and has Arts and Crafts stained-glass windows. On such a special October afternoon the church was filled with produce and flowers, which seemed to bring me even closer to Exmoor. No tea garden at Luccombe, so with more of the serendipity which my journeys are blessed, I found myself being invited to join the congregation for tea in the village hall, and there were plenty of cakes and conversation to go round. A stranger maybe, staying at Porlock that weekend, but in fact only from the other side of Somerset!

Porlock: the museum and Greencombe

Hop off the bus at Porlock and your nose should lead you to the shop and roasting-house in the yard nearby, belonging to Miles, tea and coffee merchants, who came to Porlock in 1961 from Birmingham, where they were established in 1888. The tantalising smell of roasting coffee wafts through the village each morning and anyone can book to watch this process; I am hoping that the byproduct of bean husks they gave me, which Porlock gardeners have found to be a useful mulch, will have enriched my small potager!

Porlock is a frontier village, the last and most westerly in Somerset before the famous hill, Culbone, more Exmoor and Devon. It has a fascinating history and some interesting vernacular architecture from medieval to Victorian. Porlock has a museum, had a small colony of artists and today writers and painters move here for the astonishing light and changing inspiration of the coastline and hills.

Central to all, is a village-run centre where information is dispensed with enthusiasm. Being supported by some of the businesses the reciprocity is palpable. Although Porlock now relies on visitors, there is room, if you choose the month and time, to look and wind down. Like its neighbour Minehead, Porlock also attracted a good element of émigrés who wanted to retire or holiday here and so you will see fine houses, some reminding us of Switzerland, built on the slopes and overlooking the sea.

Like St Mawes in Cornwall, Porlock shares a common protection in its topography of coast and hill, but not in aspect. Porlock is inviolate — it cannot grow. In spite of its size it caters exceedingly well for its residents and visitors. You will find another pharmacist with some original mahogany drawers with cut glass handles and gold leaf lettering and the butcher and game-dealer's shop of Clive Downs keeps its decorated tiles. I am told he makes superb pies! The assistants in the bakery are more than willing to help out with your picnic. Although the bookshop is a recent and happy addition, its stylish spaciousness gives it an air of long establishment. Another useful bastion of a small town is the hardware shop — which I hope manages to continue — and its neighbour, the double-fronted grocer's shop. Both are housed in a purpose-built late Victorian terrace, which replaced a farm. In the latter you can find everything from local broad beans to Somerset cheeses, and on the other side, for letter writers and walkers, there is a post office that is combined with outdoor clothes and shoes.

Interestingly, a photograph of 1908 shows the post office in the same position, opposite the thatched farm buildings, where smartly attired ladies are window shopping. Mr Willis, the then post master, sold tea, groceries and confectionery, linens and napery; was an agent for the Post Office Savings Bank and let out holiday apartments. Obviously there is nothing new in local businesses being multi-faceted!

The medieval Doverhay Manor, once a reading room, is now the village museum with a small herb garden, an open door and a welcoming bunch of penstemon on the table. This shining treat of a museum shows enough social history to make you want to delve deeper into the former market town, first granted a market charter in 1366 under Edward III. On the top floor there is a shepherd's crook; as many as 1,500 sheep and 200 bullocks were once penned into the main street for the fairs. There are photographs of former shops and a collection of geology, so crucial in Somerset. And a painting of the epic tale of the three-and-a-half ton lifeboat that was hauled manually over Countisbury Hill and down to Porlock Weir as it could not be launched at Lynton in the terrible storm of 1899.

The Reverend Charles E.H. Chadwyck Healey also lived in this house and commissioned its restoration from Mr Edmund Buckle. Healey speculated that it may have once been the house of the widow of crusader Sir Simon Roger, whose tomb is in the parish church. The four-light, transomed window of the hall, with the small circles of tracery, give it a churchlike character. Altered in 1883, the house fortunately has the original oak ceilings in the hall and the large stone fireplace. Once you are inside there is real sense of the Tudor period and the bonus of another unexpected view of the famous Porlock Hill and the unusual shingled spire of the parish church.

Window at Doverhay Manor

The church is named after St Dubricius, a Celtic saint who reputedly crowned King Arthur. Its west tower is thirteenth century — although the missing pinnacle blew off some 350 years ago – and interestingly the church at Culbone has a similar design, much smaller with the tower being added later. Most famous are the alabaster monuments to John Harington and his wife — some of the finest in England from the fifteenth century. The fourth Lord Harington fought for Henry V in France leading a small expedition to Agincourt for which 'he took with him eighty-six archers and twenty-nine lances'. He died only one year later in 1418, but the location is unrecorded .

Nearby, from our own time, hangs a small, embroidered memorial panel in memory of Bishop Jim of Bath and Wells. This was worked by a friend, depicting flowers seen on Exmoor, which the Bishop visited, and echoes the pale-coloured flowers in the large stained-glass panels in the Arts and Crafts style. Both the church and the majority of small vernacular buildings are constructed of sandstone, one in particular in the Drang (a lane leading to Lower Doverhay) to the east of the church is also medieval; this was once a chantry. It has wooden mullions and a rare double stable door.

In the late 1890s, the artist 'Leghe' Suthers lodged in a cottage near the church. He was one of two artists who came here to paint from Newlyn. His good friend Fred Hall had his studio in the interesting Bramdon House, now a pet shop, which has a large, stone fireplace. Both painters painted 'en plein air' — the social realism of everyday life. It was surely the stimuli and inspiration of the light and the sky effects which brought Suthers, one of the first Newlyn settlers, closely followed by Hall, to Porlock. Both exhibited at the Royal Academy. Suthers' last work, 'The Village Choir', was shown in 1905, whilst Hall's 'Porlock' was exhibited in 1890.

One hundred years later and work has just been sent to London from the forge in Doverhay where executant craftsman James Horrobin works. James was apprenticed to his father, Harry, and as a skilled draughtsman he is able to collaborate with artists and architects. James's work can be seen in Porlock, many west Somerset churches and public places within a few miles — Culbone, Minehead — but also in London and New York. His father Harry, who trained as an engineer after being stationed at Doniford in 1946, made stringed musical instruments after he retired from the forge; he died only recently at 96, surely a recommendation for keeping creative. James's passion for his work is obvious; in Porlock his public artwork at the visitor centre is a seat and a bike rack for Sustrans. His candleholders are used at the exquisite St Bartholomew, in Rodhuish, where he worked with Rachel Reckitts, and he made a round gate for the Parks in Minehead. Together with ten other local forges he has just finished a memorial screen to Sir Winston Churchill for the crypt at St Paul's Cathedral.

Allotment gate- Hallelujah Field

When Porlock was farming, every village had a blacksmith. There were farmhouses on and off the High Street as well as Lower Doverhay. I had time off last autumn at Sparkhayes Farm. I walked to Bossington

through fields and beach in one direction and to West Porlock in the other. On these beaches you can find samphire in the summer. On another walk to Hawkcombe I met the stained-glass artist Clare Maryann Green, tending her allotment in the curiously named Hallelujah Field (were these once Glebe lands?). And further up at her small cottage and studio, I saw some work in progress, much inspired by the Arts and Crafts style of the nineteenth century.

My car stood in the drive of what was once a working farm. My window framed Porlock Hill and I awoke to the sounds of the village getting about its business. And Sparkhayes provides delicious breakfasts, cooked on the Aga. It would certainly have satisfied the poets who in the 1790s, according to William Hazlitt, made their coastal walk from Nether Stowey to Lynton in one day, arriving at midnight, where they asked for and were given some 'excellent rashers of fried bacon and eggs' — and at that hour! Here 'full', (and at a civilised hour), can include: potatoes; sausages and bacon from the butcher across the road; a buffet of fruit compote or garden pears; homemade marmalade and blackberry jam in the autumn — enough to fuel any ten-mile hike!

Both Samuel Taylor Coleridge and Robert Southey, who composed a poem in the Ship during a downpour, saw Porlock. And one is tempted to read into the coastline and coombes, the imagery of Coleridge's *Kubla Khan*. We see 'dancing rocks'; we walk 'through wood and dale' and 'down to a sunless sea', which reminds us that this coast hardly sees the sun in winter.

Greencombe is a garden that really does not see the sun for two months in the winter, but it is a spring joy which Sue Lees of Mells, (chapter 1) a successful plantswoman in her own right, recommended to me years ago. One hot June day after taking the train and bus I walked out of Porlock towards Porlock Weir with the blue bay to the north and found fumitory growing in

Moon gate at Greencombe

the hedgerows. In the fields that I passed, separating the lane and sea, hay was being turned in what H.V. Morton and most of us consider, 'the delicious vale of Porlock'. You climb up to Greencombe, with Porlock Hill above and sweet-smelling roses growing wild in the hedgerow. Through a pair of white gates, the drive, then a sign which asks visitors to ring the bell. In response a strong, welcoming voice invited me to go on up. A taste of the tour which became richer by degrees.

A good garden should never reveal all at once; Greencombe

is clever in its deception. Here in stages, from the table with the bell, a path leads on up into a green amphitheatre where, as I sat talking to Greencombe's owner Miss Joan Loraine, I absorbed the colour, mood and magical situation. The first to catch my eye was a theatrical *Buddleia alternifolia*, its long twisted blooms smelling of honey; then hydrangeas, foxgloves and a striking and yet unnamed deep blue solanum.

Horace Stroud, a former councillor and merchant of Minehead, who had always wanted a garden, acquired this in 1946. He began by collecting stone from an old quarry to make the terrace and created the moon gate. He extended the original garden into what

Porlock Weir cottages

is now called the First Wood, which he rented to save it being planted with pines. He achieved the same objective with Middle Wood, where, with the help of a local gardener, he planted azaleas and rhododendrons reared from cuttings.

When Miss Loraine acquired the garden in 1966 she repaired the medieval wall, which had been part of the Porlock Deer Park. She avoided chemical sprays and mechanisation was kept to a minimum, hence the very private nature of the paths, crisscrossing the woodland. At one crossing there is a chestnut seat, felled here. Perfume is essential and here it is captivating; I just caught the fragrance of a late-flowering yellow azalea and again I caught the smell of hay being turned below.

Here a giant holly is the arboreal king, probably 400 years old, with a trunk forty-five feet in circumference. In all there are 123 native trees, including forty-three oaks, an exceptional number, when you consider that this is a private garden. In her little memoir, which is packed with planting times and successes, Miss Loraine tempts us with descriptions, such as in January, when the first perfume of winter will be *Hammamelis mollis*, the first colour, vinca, even in December.

Making this garden has been a mammoth task. They needed to eliminate the honey fungus which had invaded the woodland. This involved getting rid of over 100 giant tree stumps which occasionally needed dynamite. They enriched the thin soil with leaf mould, spreading between twenty-five and thirty tons of compost a year, which feeds blooms and suppresses weeds. Over the years Miss Loraine has carefully built up the national collection of Polystichum, Gaultheria, Vaccinium, (blueberries, or wurts as they are called on Exmoor) and Erythronium.

Even in the vegetable garden Greencombe's intimate mood continues, where brick paths are laid for winter work and seats are placed in a corner. I wallowed in the light and scent that the first day of summer brings. This one will be their sixtieth.

The Culbone effect

Of all the journeys in this collection Culbone needs time — because of its hidden location, because time appears to have stood still and for Culbone's stilling quality. Over the last 200 years visitors, writers, artists, painters, poets, potters and natural historians have been deeply affected by the *genius loci* of the tiny hamlet. Thus it has become endowed with a mystical legacy.

On a warm August morning an accommodating driver, who might still have been in the 1920s, pre-car-driving society, drove us up the famous Porlock Hill with 'a sensation of having been shot several hundred feet higher in a matter of moments', exactly as Sylvia Townsend Warner described. There was a mass intake of breath as we waited for an oncoming truck at one bend, and more wonder as we looked back at the beauty of Porlock Bay, Hurlestone Point and Selworthy Beacon.

The story of Coleridge's supposed stay at Ash Farm, *Kubla Khan* and the view that the romantic visionary, Samuel Palmer painted of Culbone church were in my mind when, with a good friend, who knows Culbone, I planned this expedition. Our first destination was Ash Farm, to which we walked after taking the 'summer coach' from Porlock.

Because of the apocryphal person-from-Porlock story, I wanted to see Ash Farm, where Coleridge was supposed to have rested, when having walked from his home at Nether Stowey he was unwell. After taking opium he dreamed. It is said that his recollection and the transposition to verse of a drug-induced dream, were interrupted by someone knocking at his door and an announcement by the farmer, or his wife, that 'a person from Porlock' had arrived to see him. After an hour of what was seemingly unimportant conversation, Coleridge was no longer able to write down any more than fifty-four lines of *Kubla Khan*, in which his dream had transported him to the denizens of Xanadu.

These beautiful and haunting words are embedded in the public psyche — to the extent that short extracts were cleverly extracted by James Lees-Milne for some of his autobiographic titles: *Caverns of Ice, A Mingled Measure* and *Prophesying Peace* being just three.

With the sea ahead, tantalisingly blue, heather-covered banks and hills, we walked; the fattening rumps of the lambs, stamped with JR, led us to Yearner and Ash Farms, owned by the Richards family for three generations. And how long, I wonder, have the successive generations of house martins been circling and feeling their wings and tails above Yearner Farm? As some appeared to be practising for the long haul back, the last clutch were still crying for food in their round mud nests. Every year the long-awaited arrival is as humbling and mysterious as the last departure.

Tony and John Richards gave their time, inviting us into the flagstoned farmhouse for a cup of tea; our own 'hour' passed too quickly. Ash Farm has always provided wayfarers with bed and breakfast, like so many west country farms, as a way of life and means of meeting the world beyond the moor. Their cool kitchen reminded me of staying on farms in Cornwall which years ago only had a pig but where the simple supper table had a whole roast chicken for two and two dishes of vegetables. And I remembered seeing the cream being scalded for the following day. We talked of the old days when farmers could serve milk and cream from the house cow to their guests — now forbidden; of 'set aside' and Tony's unfertilised buttercup and clover-filled field, which we crossed to Culbone Combe. The Richards know Exmoor well and are well known for their walling skills; as there is little material here the earth banks are only faced with the stone.

And inevitably we pondered the whole Coleridge episode; was Ash Farm the location for the interruption? In the Crewe manuscript the poet described writing his 'fragment' in a farmhouse a quarter of a mile from Culbone, but there is no mention of an interruption. Was it Withycombe Farm, as Tony Richards believes, now a ruin? As both are equidistant from Culbone it could have been either. But isn't it better left unsolved?

Nothing had prepared me for the sight of the church, pale with whitewashed walls glinting in the sunlight — encircled by an amphitheatre of trees. I was drawn immediately to an unusual oaken half-stable door, designed to keep animals away; a porch and a simple double-plank door with whole-width brackets opening into a tiny nave with oak pews and a family box pew. There is a wagon roof and a rood screen and the untrammelled peace of this space is embellished simply with a red and gold reredos, designed by C.F.A. Voysey for Lady Lovelace in 1928, and a pair of candlesticks made by blacksmith James Horrobin down at Doverhay. With two vases of country flowers — alchemilla and a few stems of the August-abundant montbretia — and the visitors book. Culbone needs no more than contemplation.

The history of Culbone church, reputedly the smallest in the country is chequered. It is named after St Culban; a Celtic saint. A slate spire rests on the nave, added after 1835. There may be some Norman stonework in the chancel; and the north wall has an old window with oak mullions and tracery, with a smaller, squint window below. In the churchyard near the yew there is a preaching cross and an engraving of 1800 shows another cottage beyond this. Culbone was as much affected by the Black Death as most of Somerset, but this special situation was also, over hundreds of years, the home of outcasts, lepers and Indian charcoal burners. Surely the sum of people from every country past and present, every skill proud and humble has added to the weight of Culbone's uncommon potency.

When Palmer painted his view of Culbone looking down through the valley there were fifty-six people living in eleven houses, by 1891, only thirty-one. Today, apart from the barn, or former pottery, just two cottages keep the church company. But in 1770 a market cross was set up and open-air markets took place three times a year, though not in winter.

Both Richard Warner in 1796 and the naturalist William George Maton around 1794 came here, and it is interesting to compare their accounts from the discursive to the sublime. The latter, a fellow of the Linnaean Society, observed scenery and antiquities at the height of the picturesque movement. Walking up from West Porlock, he saw the eminence above the hanging woods of beech with elm, oak and crags — giving an 'uncommon richness and luxuriance of effect'. He was drawn to the thicket in search of botanical produce and found rare plants such as *Bynum verticulum* and *Lichen cochleatus*. When he reached romantic Culbone, he saw the village in a narrow cove 'about four hundred feet above the sea', and the Welsh Mountains, which loom surprisingly close on a fine day. In sunlight his Culbone was a spectacle that 'exhibits beauty and sublimity united to a surprising and enchanting degree'.

Warner called Culbone 'Lilliputian'. He too found the spot conducive to meditation with the deep murmur of the sea beyond, contrasting this peaceful picture with an anecdote, told to him by a blacksmith, of Culbone revels in the 1750s, which must have coincided with a market. Before the Acts of Enclosure these activities were common occurrences and at least 300 people had gathered in the churchyard. Flustered with ale and warmed with dancing, the blacksmith gambled, losing too much. With the imminent arrival of another mouth to feed, he told Warner he resolved to win back all his losses and never to gamble again, a vow he kept for forty-five years! In 1821 one of the cottages actually became a public house called the Fox and Hounds, selling beer and cider, no doubt, until around 1875.

The refreshment that the Cooks provided in their cottage for over sixty years was less intoxicating. Ernest was born and had lived in the cottage near the church since the 1890s. Lizzie came from Cornwall, married him in 1914 and lived on here until she died in 1980. As their cottage lay directly on the right of way, now the South West Coastal Path from Silcombe Farm, (which also provides bed and breakfast), Mrs Cook considered she was duty bound to open. So the back door always was, the fire burned and the kettle simmered ready on the hob. I was told that her welcome was as generous for her regulars as it was for visitors, for whom she provided a tea of home-made cake and jam. Only one sign told of their existence: a flat stone on the Porlock Weir path inscribed with the message 'Teas', which some sceptical visitors, taking what appeared to be the route to nowhere, found difficult to believe.

Whilst Lizzie Cook dispensed teas, new neighbours arrived who became firm friends. In 1950 the potter Waistel Cooper, originally a painter and born in 1921 in Scotland, returned from Iceland where he had become 'hooked on clay'. At Culbone he resolved to isolate himself in order to explore and experiment with various materials. He set up his pottery at the gatehouse above the church to develop glazes that were given texture through the use of ash — from dried, burnt and sieved clippings of bramble, nettles, weeds and bracken. Joan and Waistel Cooper showed their pots on the terraces they had hewn out of the hill, where he wrote in 1956 'each piece looks as if it grew out of the soil'. Cooper loved the golden clay that came from Broomstreet further up the hill. Thus the only commodity they 'imported' was oil from Porlock, but according to

Worthy Toll

Rosemary Burnett, her father gave Cooper his motorbike so that he could transport large pots up and down to Culbone!

Some hours and a picnic later my friend and I descended the new path and saw and heard the murmuring sea over the level tops of the trees; the original has been diverted. Much of the planting was carried out by Lord Lovelace, who was passionate about trees. At the Worthy Toll House we came down to earth. Here Rosemary Burnett lived and collected the toll money in the 1950s. One of her successors Judith Sparks, is still opening the gate!

As part of the journey I wanted to see if any of the work that

Voysey had done on this estate was still visible. He designed the village hall at Porlock. The connection between Voysey and the Lovelaces began in the late 1890s when he designed an inn and cottages on their estate at Elmesthorp in Leicestershire, followed by work in Surrey. What is not completely clear is whether the cottages at Culbone are all his or the result of collaboration with Lady Lovelace, herself a designer. Whilst the cottage opposite the church has some Voysey-ish eaves and buttresses, the cottage west of the church shows an imported Surrey characteristic in one of its brick barley-twist chimneys. Perhaps this was by Lady Lovelace? His alterations and additions at Worthy, just seen from the road, were a chimney, a new hall and staircase, together with new windows, in 1916. Lady Lovelace also commissioned him to design the beautiful memorial stone seat for her husband which overlooks Culbone churchyard.

The ripples emanating from Culbone will without doubt continue to effect many people in many walks of life for years, but it was now late afternoon as we climbed down to the weir. With the sun still on our backs, we walked along the road through West Porlock and then reached Porlock itself.

Boats 'splaundered' at Porlock Weir

Selected reading list:

Ashton, Rosemary, 1996, *Life of Samuel Taylor Coleridge*
Ball, Allan, 2001, *Somerset Illustrated: The county's heritage in prints and drawings*
Barlow, Frank, 1974, *The Feudal Kingdom of England, 1042–1216*
Barrett, C.R.B., 1994, *Somersetshire; highways, byways and waterways*
Betty, J.H., 1997, *Rural Life in Wessex 1500–1900*
Blackmore, R.D., 1869, *Lorna Doone*
Burton, S.H.A., 1975, *West Country Anthology*
Chadwyck Healey, Charles E.H., 1901, *The History of Part of West Somerset*
Clark, Evelyn V., 1933, *Walter Raymond the man - his work and letters*
Cooper, Cicily, 1966, *Memoirs of Selwothy and West Somerset*
Cottle, Joseph, 1847, *Reminiscences of Samuel Taylor Coleridge*
Cumming, E. & Kaplan, W., 1991, *The Arts and Crafts Movement*
Defoe, Daniel, 1971 edn., *A Tour Through the Whole Island of Great Britain*
Dixon, Roger & Muthesius, Stefan, 1991, *Victorian Architecture*
Goodhart-Rendel, H.S., 1953, *English Architecture since the Regency*
Hardy, Thomas, 1903, *A Laodicean*
Hartley, Dorothy, 1964, *Food in England*
Hartley, Dorothy, 1979, *The Land of England*
Hazlitt, William, 1949 edn., *The Essays of William Hazlitt*
Hole, Christina, 1950, *English Custom and Usage*
Holmes, Richard, 1989, *Coleridge: Early Visions*
Hoskins, W.G., 1965, *The Making of the English Landscape*
Knight, Francis A., 1909, *Cambridge County Geologies, Somerset*
Lawrence, Berta, 1951, *A Somerset Journal*
Lawrence, Berta, 1952, *Quantock Country*
Lea, Herman, 1903, *Thomas Hardy's Wessex*
Little, Bryan, 1983, *Portrait of Somerset*
Lovett Turner, M., 1949, *Somerset*
Mais, S.P.B., 1946, *This Unknown Island*
Maton, William George, 1794–6, *Observations on the Western Counties of England*, vol 11
McGarvie, Michael, 1980, *Castle Cary*
Morton, H.V.,1936, *In Search of England*
Palmer, Kingsley, 1976, *The Folklore of Somerset*
Pevsner, Nikolaus, 1958, *The Buildings of England: North Somerset, South and West Somerset*
Powys, John, 1932, *A Glastonbury Romance*
Raymond, Walter, 1921, *Somerset and her Folk Movement*
Richardson, A.E., 1935, *The Inns of England*
Waite, Vincent, 1964, *Quantock Country*
Warner, Richard, 1800, *A Walk Through Some of the Western Counties of England*
Warner, Richard, 1826, *A History of the Abbey of Glastonbury and the Town*
Warner, Sylvia Townsend, 1949, *Somerset*
Wedlake, A.I., 1973, *History of Watchet*
Woodforde, James, 1981–4 edn.,*The Diary of a Country Parson 1758–1802*

216

221

223

List of Illustrations

18th Century shoes and buckles p96 with kind permission of Clark's International.